Public Interest
and the
Business of Broadcasting

Public Interest and the Business of Broadcasting

THE BROADCAST INDUSTRY LOOKS AT ITSELF

Edited by
Jon T. Powell
Wally Gair

Q

QUORUM BOOKS
New York • Westport, Connecticut • London

Library of Congress Cataloging-in-Publication Data

Public interest and the business of broadcasting : the broadcast
industry looks at itself / edited by Jon T. Powell and Wally Gair.
   p. cm.
  Bibliography: p.
  Includes index.
  ISBN 0–89930–198–3 (lib. bdg. : alk. paper)
  1. Television programs, Public interest—Law and legislation—
United States. 2. Radio programs, Public interest—Law and
legislation—United States. I. Powell, Jon T. II. Gair, Wally.
KF2805.P83 1988
343.73'09945—dc19
[347.3039945]   88–3098

British Library Cataloguing in Publication Data is available.

Library of Congress Catalog Card Number: 88–3098
ISBN: 0–89930–198–3

First published in 1988 by Quorum Books

Greenwood Press, Inc.
88 Post Road West, Westport, Connecticut 06881

Printed in the United States of America

The paper used in this book complies with the
Permanent Paper Standard issued by the National
Information Standards Organization (Z39.48–1984).

10 9 8 7 6 5 4 3 2 1

CONTENTS

PREFACE

This book is not intended to be an exhaustive analysis of the public-interest concept in broadcasting; neither is it a treatise on reform measures. It is presented as a cross section of theoretical and pragmatic perceptions as described by successful broadcast professionals—and those who work with them—about the role of public interest in commercial broadcasting. The articles range from a comprehensive legal analysis to reporting of personal philosophies and experiences related to public interest.

The intent of this book is to offer candid and genuine descriptions of what the public-interest obligation actually means to the practitioner. Some contributors give specific details concerning actual broadcast activities that fulfill the public-interest obligation. Others are strongly critical about the intrusion of the public-interest concept as interpreted by the federal government into the operation of commercial broadcasting. In all instances, however, the writers depict the realities they perceive in their own words. A brief description of each contributor's professional activities is included to provide additional perspective for each article.

This book is divided into three general areas: The Broad View; In The Marketplace; and Other Views. Following the editors' introduction, in the lead article under the first general heading, a former FCC chairman provides a personal and general retrospective of the public interest concept. This is followed by a detailed study describing how public interest has been legislated by Congress and litigated in the courts. Next, national broadcast leaders and network executives describe how they each perceive the role of public interest in broadcasting. This is followed by the individual reflections of large-, small-, and medium-market broadcasters. The remaining articles of the book are contributed by executives who use radio and television as part of their professional work. In the introductory and concluding essays the editors offer additional perspectives.

Perhaps some of the examples described will prove useful. We sincerely hope that the ideas contained throughout this book will increase understanding and stimulate discussion about that most challenging of all trusts for the commercial broadcaster—the public interest.

About the Editors

JON T. POWELL is a Professor of Communication Studies and Instructional Technology at Northern Illinois University, DeKalb. He is the author of *International Broadcasting by Satellite* (Quorum Books, 1985). His articles have appeared in such scholarly and professional journals as *Law and Contemporary Problems, Federal Communications Bar Journal, Advertising Law Anthology, Media and Methods, Supervisory Management,* and *Personnel Journal.*

WALLY GAIR has spent his working life in and around the broadcast media. From his first job as a newswriter at a radio station in Peoria, Illinois, to his past eight years as Executive Director of the Illinois Broadcasters Association, Gair has been involved in virtually every aspect of broadcasting. For the past eight years, he has also written and edited the monthly newsletter of the IBA, *The Transmitter.*

Public Interest
and the
Business of Broadcasting

INTRODUCTION

Some time ago, a scholar in the field of political science made an extensive investigation into the concepts of public interest. At the conclusion of this detailed, carefully constructed, and systematic study of the general concept of public interest, he noted that: "It may be somewhat difficult for some readers to accept the conclusion that there is no public-interest theory worthy of the name and that the concept itself is significant primarily as a datum of politics."[1] While the concept of public interest may indeed be vague at times—and it might be considered most useful to keep it that way—its implementation by the broadcast industry in response to congressional mandate and ongoing FCC regulations is far from vague or theoretical.

As you will see, the legal obligations of the broadcast licensee have been translated into local activities, community efforts, personal involvement, and sound business practice. The purpose of this introduction is not to discuss the legal ramifications of public interest for the broadcaster—that is well done by the contributors—but to offer some perspectives on this principle. Although the public-interest obligation can be described in a host of ways depending on whether one is addressing a government, social, or business organization, it has special significance for the broadcaster. After all, if broadcasting is public communication, it must serve the interests of listeners and viewers. Otherwise it is not serving the public interest. In other words, the obligation of public interest for the broadcaster is driven primarily by what interests the public. Only by following the dictates of the listening and viewing public can the broadcaster survive economically because for broadcaster, like print publisher, the U.S. marketplace of ideas functions first as a marketplace where consumer choice remains the major force.

Beyond the marketplace, however, exists federal regulation. The broadcaster must operate his service with both in mind. Under such circumstances, the broadcaster must confront a coalition of federal mandates, public obligations, and the competitive demands of the marketplace. Public interest becomes, therefore, a practical matter of responding to what interests that public *and* what federal regulation requires. The broadcaster must look both ways. As a result, good business practice for the broadcaster means responding to specific community needs, acting to interest and serve the listening or viewing community.

What comes to mind when you think of "public interest" and broadcasting? It might be the thirty- or sixty-second spots for radio and television knows as PSA's, or public service announcements. These spots run the gamut from urging the use of seat belts to controlling teenage pregnancy and curtailing the slaughter on our highways caused by drunk drivers. It might also be what Public Broadcasting stations do, since they perform a different function by catering to smaller, more selective audiences.

What else comes to mind when the flag of public interest is raised? Before you read further, forget your old concepts about what public interest really means to the professionals. While the activities mentioned above are truly part and parcel of what America has grown used to seeing and hearing since broadcasting began, there are a variety of other services that they regularly perform. The contributors to this book illustrate well that variety from the small community to the large, from the individual perspective to the corporate, from the social to the political.

The public-interest obligation of the broadcaster was first formally identified by law in 1927 and reaffirmed in 1934 by Congress. While the later additions to the public interest obligation of the fairness doctrine, equal time, and other concepts to be explained later in this book, had their basis in law and regulation, the federal government has at times changed its stance. Whatever changes have been made, broadcasters continue to consider the application of public interest both as a legal requirement and sound business practice.

Beyond this, the radio or television station is seen as an integral part of the community. What may have begun as a legal concept has evolved into a social one. In a very real sense, the broadcaster has become so much a part of the community that one cannot separate one from the other. Whether you live in a large city or a small town, the radio or television station located there is part of the identification one has with the character of that locality.

When we talk of "community," we often mean the way a community looks at itself—and that self-image is developed in part by the local role assumed by the broadcaster with the result that the concept of public interest becomes more than a legal definition. It assumes social and, perhaps most important, personal dimensions. The descriptions of the public-interest activities in this book reveal that broadcast stations can go beyond programming, beyond public service announcements, to become vital and integral contributors—indeed partners—in community efforts to support and improve the local quality of life.

Some conclusions can be drawn from the application of the public-interest concept on a local basis. Although the term is vague but value-intensive, it still serves as a guiding principle made specific by community needs. The presence of federal law and regulation serves to motivate the broadcaster to seek ways of translating its vagueness into a concrete record of contribution to the community's welfare. The public-interest concept thus becomes useful when it can produce clear, identifiable results for the broadcast station's record, its logs, its application for license renewal. Raising money, sponsoring safety campaigns, and creating public awareness of important social problems constitute the results of the broadcasters' efforts to convert a vague term into a concrete act. Furthermore, in most instances these efforts, far from being of the "one time only" kind, become an ongoing commitment, a continuing involvement.

There is another side as well to the issues of public interest. There is also always the restraint of what is *not* in the public interest. The broadcast station in programming and advertising routinely finds itself in a position of judging what is acceptable and what is not, based on the public—and "public" most often means "community"—interest.

Whatever else is said about the concept of public interest, it does not exist in a vacuum. It remains part and parcel of the *commercial* marketplace and the community. It functions in a competitive environment. The tension between "public" and "private" interests will continue regardless as long as the U.S. broadcasting system remains chiefly commercial, where survival means profit and where the advertiser is interested primarily in the size of the audience for the commercial message.

Another observation should be made about the broadcaster's general role of community communicator. If public interest is to have any basic meaning, it must be found in the *unique* role of the broadcaster. The examples provided by this book's contributors underscore the special role of the broadcaster. The public interest concept becomes particularly useful because broadcasters can accomplish community goals that cannot be accomplished in any other way.

In an attempt to provide perspective to the articles that follow, we will briefly describe the cultural revolution spawned by the electronic media; the concept of television as the ultimate "melting pot" of American society; how radio and television has brought America together in times of great national crisis and tragedy; how it has changed our outlook on the way, and how it may reveal more than we realize about who we think we are. All this in the name of public interest! We will look beyond the coverage of news and public affairs programming to examine how regular entertainment programming— especially our sitcoms—give us an American identity that helped break down regionalism in America.

We will also explore what those in and associated with broadcasting think and feel about public interest. Some of our contributors will be expressing views that have not been heard before. We have attempted to give the reader a pragmatic view, broad in scope—not from the usual lineup of academicians and politicians, but from a varied group including a former FCC chairman, a local television station sales manager, small- and large-market broadcast executives,and some who, while they are not actual broadcasters, have had extensive and continuing work with the broadcast industry in advertising and public service. But first, some perspectives.

The Golden Age and Kids and Some Thoughts on Censorship

Television has often been castigated for its lack of good programming for children, a criticism that seems at times all too well founded. Unfortunately those behind the criticism want to bring about changes by government action, which in the view of the authors impinges greatly upon constitutional rights.

Broadcasting has not always overlooked specific programming for children. In what has come to be known as the Golden Age of Radio (1930s–1950s) children's programming constituted an important part of the network schedule. Perhaps as a result of this programming— along with the experiences created by an economic depression and a world war—children of that generation were presented with a set of values to live by, values that were not government-mandated but products of the marketplace at its best. Working together, networks and advertisers turned out programs that would entertain, educate, and enthuse their youthful audience. The mixture also managed to sell a product and who among us who lived in that era were injured by urging our mothers to buy Ovaltine, Wheaties, Orange Crush, or Wonder Bread? All the while we were being entertained and "pitched" to we were receiving messages of loyalty, sportsmanship, and good citizenship. Who among us did not have our eyes opened to the world around us in a time of great national isolationism as Jack Armstrong roamed the globe with his Uncle Jim to strange-sounding places like Manila, Macao, and the jungles of Asia and Africa? The Lone Ranger was given to anger only when his trusted friend was in danger from outlaws. And his trusted friend was not a white man but an American Indian, that most maligned of groups, especially in the movies of the day, so that some of us learned another lesson of tolerance and equality. Most of us learned that crime did not pay from Dick Tracy or Superman or the Green Hornet or even the scarlet-coated Mountie from north of the border, Sergeant Preston of the Yukon.

We ate our Wheaties and drank our Ovaltine, and we were informed and entertained. No Big Brother here, watching and censoring. The networks and advertising agencies censored themselves. We were not and are not a perfect society. Many of those who listened to those radio shows and heard those preachings of justice, equality and loyalty, did not heed the words. So killers, robbers, rapists, and bigots came from that era. Radio did not, of course, resolve all the problems created by antisocial behavior, but it made a contribution to the development of youthful values.

What concerns there were in those days about the quality of programming in no way matched what was to come with the advent of television. This all leads us to a brief discussion of the nature of censorship and why it cannot be an answer to any perceived problems with broadcasting.

The opening phrase of the First Amendment, "Congress shall make no law...," clearly establishes a basic principle in simple phrases not found in any other national constitution despite the fact that many countries have used our Constitution as a model for their own. Beyond setting clear legal limits for official intervention in the expression or exchange of information, the First Amendment firmly delineates the relationship between the government and the governed.

Most of the controversy over programming, be it on radio or television, involves what should *not* be aired. Most broadcasters have their favorite stories of controversial programs, or statements, or even words that have gone out over the airwaves to draw adverse reaction from the public. And it goes the other way as well. That is, the market is tested first to see if there would be any strong objection to a program's subject matter or a particular product. There is nothing particularly unusual about a broadcaster pulling a commercial or not airing a program in the community. Like the local newspaper publisher, the broadcaster is exercising judgment about the effect of a program and, if warranted, the right to keep that program off the air.

Depending on the group that wants that commercial or story or program aired, such an act is "censorship." It is not. Unfortunately, the term "censorship" has been used so loosely in this country that any and all acts of "prior restraint" (keeping something from being published or aired) are so labeled. However, under our Constitution, the document that determines the structure and operation of our government, only the government is precluded from exercising prior restraint. The private citizen, involved in publishing or broadcasting, can withhold, can exercise prior restraint with immunity. Of course, the broadcaster remains responsible for what is aired and will be held accountable for slander, public safety, and other such matters.

The point here, however, is that censorship accurately identifies the relationship between the government and the private citizen by forbidding the government from taking action to keep a citizen from exercising freedom of expression. Whatever the private publisher or broadcaster does to preclude publication or airing should be given another term because they are not—and properly so in this country— part of the government. In this context, the broadcaster is left with the uneasy task of pleasing the community audience, answering to federal regulation, and operating a business. It was easier and simpler in the early days of radio.

Radio and the War

The heritage of the public-interest role of broadcasters finds its strongest expression during World War II. Radio served to keep us informed. Radio first brought us face to face with the realities of war through the early broadcasts of Ed Murrow from London during the blitz and the report of George Putnam on a ship headed for Normandy and the D-Day invasion of Europe. But radio's greatest contribution was to home-front morale.

It was radio that helped make light of meat and gas rationing through the jokes of Bob Hope and the rapier wit of Fred Allen. Radio urged housewives to save fat and drippings, so that they could be turned into soap. Radio asked us to conserve rubber and collect paper and scrap, all needed for the war effort. It was the laughter generated by Jack Benny, Fibber McGee and Molly, Edgar Bergen and Charlie McCarthy that helped us get through the dark days of 1942 and 1943.

It was radio that encouraged enlistments in the armed forces while parading its own stars off to war in front of its audiences. Whenever a major star left a show to go into service, it was done with some fanfare.

Radio reacted to war the way the nation as a whole did. The story lines reflected the changes—Superman tracked Nazis instead of two- bit hoods, Ma Perkins's son went off to war, gold stars were placed on the windows of soap opera heroines, and news broadcasts became a national obsession.

Radio became an instrument of persuasion. Propaganda became a weapon. The Nazis refined its use under propaganda minister Joseph Goebbels. The Goebbels version of what was going on in Germany differed greatly from reality. In the United States, propaganda took on many forms. Movie propaganda portrayed our enemies as completely ruthless, blond crew-cut animals in jackboots, or as toothy, smirking bespectacled killers of women and children. This was done to encourage hatred for the enemy, so that we would fight harder, build planes faster, and save and conserve without complaint.

Radio played its part in this effort. The enemies changed from outlaws to "Japs" and Nazis. Soap opera characters were urged to save soap, use foods other than meat, which was scarce, and generally accept the restricted life-style. Children were encouraged to save paper and collect scrap iron and tin. They were taught to recognize silhouettes of planes, just in case the enemy ever breached our air space. Those on the home front were made to feel just as important as those on the war fronts.

During the war and forever after, radio, like Americans in general, lost much of its innocence. We began to face real problems. Radio, reflecting society, was timid about broaching such sensitive issues as intolerance and racism. The Lone Ranger had done it subtly as had the Green Hornet. Of course, the word "racism" was never used, nor as a matter of fact were "black" or "Negro" as we continued to sweep that American shame under the rug.

But small efforts were made. When people with strange-sounding foreign names moved into the "Bible belt" Rushville Center, Ma Perkins stood up to be counted. Ma stood up and denounced bigotry, just as she had dispensed her other wisdoms for so many years on two networks for the makers of Oxydol. It wasn't Abe Lincoln, but it wasn't bad. It was a start.

During the war and afterwards, radio served the national public interest in assisting the war effort, creating a sense of national purpose, and in the end, addressing problems that needed exposure, even if it was meek or indirect. As the war ended, radio helped us to look at ourselves through fictional portrayals. We were given a clearer perspective of the problems individuals faced as the country turned from war to peace, and Johnny came marching home.

Television: A New Era

Soon after the World War II ended, the country began to gear up for the production of civilian goods and the expansion of services.

And a great revolution was to take place in broadcasting, a revolution where public interest became a matter of sight, sound, and motion in the living room.

Just before the war (in 1939) those who attended the New York World's Fair had been treated to a startling look at the World of Tomorrow. But that tomorrow was delayed by the war. One of those glimpses of tomorrow was offered at the RCA exhibit. In a large room resembling a studio of some sort, a band was perched on a stage with a female vocalist at a microphone—nothing really startling about that—but when fair-goers walked into another room, the most amazing thing happened. They saw on a screen exactly what was taking place in the other room. For those spectators this was their first look at a new miracle, television. Audiences had seen inklings of television in movies featuring Buck Rogers and Flash Gordon, but that was fantasy reserved for the planet Mongo and Saturday movie matinees.

In 1947, the 1939 World's Fair electronic experiment graduated to a black and white reality. Store windows in the big eastern cities displayed television sets, and curious crowds gathered in the streets to witness the miracle.

The programs were few, the broadcast day short, and production crude by today's standards, but it was a beginning. With the introduction of coaxial cable a few years later, the miracle became a coast-to-coast marvel. An industry was born. This young upstart was misunderstood by many of its own. It was criticized by those whose own medium of advertising would have to face new competition for the advertising dollar. And television was wholeheartedly embraced by the American public.

Public interest was no longer confined to the ear. The viewer could witness an event first-hand from the safety and comfort of the living room. No professional observer was needed except to clarify or amplify the event, and given the circumstances, even that might not be necessary. Public interest was taking on new dimensions, new significance. Words, though still important, would forever be only part of the public's experience.

Television As American Culture

"Democracy was conceived in an unwired world," Benjamin Barber has observed.[2] However, this democratic process underwent dramatic change with the advent of television. If the concept of public interest was ever to play a significant role in broadcasting, television by its very nature assured that role a preeminent status.

Television, much like radio before it, has been criticized for the homogeneity of its programs, seemingly aimed at a teenage mentality.

The authors, however, agree with Barber that "network television's homogenized programming benefited democracy: By offering the country the semblance of national culture and national political norms, it provided a consensus indispensable to national unity."[3] Such influence lends significance to the broadcaster's public interest obligation and makes it all the more apparent.

Public interest and national unity have been fused occasionally as a direct result of network attention: in the 1950s with integration, the 1960s with John Kennedy and Vietnam, the 1970s with Watergate. As Barber describes the phenomenon:

> But more often, the television consensus was informal and indirect—national debates such as the Kennedy–Nixon exchanges, national media personalities such as Ed Sullivan, Johnny Carson and Walter Cronkite, and such national rituals as the Kennedy funeral, the moon walk, and the mourning for Martin Luther King—all these bestowed upon the country a legacy of national symbols and myths that cut across our divisive regions, our sects, interest groups, parties, races, ethnic communities and political constituencies.[4]

Such influence, if not in the public interest and serving the public, could have been most harmful. The sight, sound, and motion of network television programming offered in similar fashion national and international events to living-room audiences who, despite their cultural and political pluralism, could accept them in a spirit of sharing. One can reasonably assume that as a whole, the print media with its reliance on printed symbols, could not match television for stirring imagination and directing emotions toward common goals. As Barber wrote, "If there is an American melting pot, it is fired nowadays primarily by electronic means."[5]

From the beginning, the philosophy of federal regulation over broadcasting has been based on the perception of a local service. While this is certainly true for radio, which had its national influence until the 1950s, the high cost of television programming mandated national distribution as soon as possible. Thus, the public-interest issues of television have come to be mostly national issues, and most radio controversies are local, sometimes regional in character. However, that is not to say that television's social effects are somehow so broad that they can only be considered in a general social context. Nothing could be further from the truth. Television is personal, as personal as the living room in which it is received, as personal as the individual viewer who feels elated or angered by a program or personality, or who falls asleep. Perhaps the most significant contribution of television to public interest has been to create a growing sensitivity to fellow human beings.

Obviously, the power of television has both national and personal dimensions. In its national dimension, it has most effectively translated broad social movements and deep social attitudes into individual messages, which have reached into the privacy and security of home. Television has shown us "Who we are in common and what we see in common."[6]

Society as Seen in the Tube: Reflections in the Public Interest

Broadcasting can either lead and form public taste and opinion, or follow public taste, depending on your outlook. Chances are, it does both—sometimes simultaneously—because while it forms taste for some where none or little exists, for others it is reflecting the same. Such an observation is never clear-cut. Two or more viewers often see the same event or character in two or more different ways.

When Archie Bunker looses his diatribe against minorities, Jews, Catholics, or Democrats, viewers who like him can feel a kinship. On the other hand, those who disagree with the Bunker mentality watch and laugh, pointing out how these foolish responses reveal themselves so clearly for what they are. Liberals and conservatives alike can watch "All in the Family" and reinforce their viewpoints.

Like real life, good television allows for personal growth in a character, even if it's ever so little. So Archie, a racist, can host a famous black celebrity like Sammy Davis, Jr., in his cab and in his home and brag about it. Now, Archie did not suddenly become color-blind. He simply looked at Davis as a black who is different—*not unlike our real-life attitudes*. When viewed over the years Archie's metamorphosis, after being harassed by wife, daughter, and son-in-law, seems to tell us something about ourselves. We have the opportunity through comedy to witness our foolishness when prejudice replaces good sense and social ethics.

Most of our television characters have ancestral roots in their characters from radio or television. Archie's was surely a branch of the Ralph Kramden family. Ralph did not have a political philosophy, but like Archie, he was convinced that he knew all the answers. Like Archie, he felt he was the king of his household. Like Bunker, Kramden was loud, coarse, at heart a spoiled child. Both Archie and Ralph bellowed at and attempted to intimidate their wives.

Today as television reflects society, neither Alice Kramden nor Edith Bunker would react in the manner they did in their respective eras. Edith was on the cutting edge of the feminist movement and began to change in later shows just as women all over the country were changing. She began to stand up to Archie, to speak her own mind and express her thoughts instead of merely mimicking her husband's. If Alice Kramden, a childless woman, were to appear in the New Honeymooners, most certainly she would not spend her entire day cooking and cleaning the sparse Kramden apartment. She would be in the work force, pursuing a career.

What can be said about these observations that has not already been explained? Perhaps one thing more should be mentioned. These examples have, for the most part been part of the entertainment provided by network television. To succeed, the programs had first to attract audiences and then to hold them week after week, sometimes year after year. Beyond the obvious writing, acting, and production talent needed to sustain such enterprises, it seems almost inevitable that good entertainment also teaches. Public interest, therefore, relates not only to the specific enterprises you will find described in this book, but to the whole body of television, from Archie Bunker to Bill Cosby, from Ralph Kramden to Ben Cartwright, from Ed Sullivan to Frank Reynolds.

Whether television leads or follows public tastes and attitudes—and it does both—it does so most often through experiences the audience finds satisfying. To survive in the marketplace, the broadcaster must first build an audience; then comes the message, the opportunity to explore new ideas and shape attitudes.

But the risk up front for the broadcaster, however dedicated to the public interest, is that the audience at home can say "that's for me ... or not for me." Failure to succeed with programming, good, bad, or indifferent, is still failure. It took three years of considerable effort to get "All in the Family" into the broadcast schedule because of its obviously controversial subject matter. Fortunately, someone had the foresight to see its potential, and the rest is history. Otherwise it could still be sitting on the shelf. Was that decision to air it in the public interest? Most would say yes. In the beginning, however, it was a business decision, a risk taken in the belief that a sufficient number of Americans would enjoy watching it. The network executives who made that decision did so for business reasons. And why not? That is how it works in the American system of commercial broadcasting, and in that context only can the issue of public interest be properly understood.

In an article in *Channels*, William Henry III, writing of Ralph Kramden, points out, "They exaggerated normal human behavior just enough to enable people who cannot laugh at themselves to believe they were laughing at someone else—while letting the rest of us recognize the all too familiar excesses of our temperaments."[7] It is clear that broadcast programming for the most part succeeds because it entertains. Is this in the public interest? From the broadcaster's viewpoint, because the size of the audience measures the success of the program, public interest is first served because the public is interested, and the industry, therefore, survives financially. To take this thought one step further, can entertainment itself be considered in the public interest beyond the fact that it serves to keep some in front of a television set and out of mischief? Can we both cheer for the point of view acted out in a sitcom and still grow intellectually or socially? Many think yes, and in the long run we are better for it. Obviously we do not watch to learn; we learn because we watch. We watch to be entertained, to laugh, or cry. But if the residual effect is there, then television has become more than a source of laughter or tears, it has become an instrument for the transmission of ideas and ideals—not a small task for any medium with public interest obligations.

In his book *Post Conservative America* Kevin Phillips writes that the United States will soon be menaced by a type of fascism inflicted on us by a populist lower-middle-class conservatism. This conservatism will show itself in hatred of the rich and the poor, resulting in a search for a strong man on a horse to restore (by force if necessary) the American way of life. Playing a part in this will be an increased desire for cultural and moral traditionalism and nationalistic pride.[8]

Can this happen as long as our popular television shows play to a different set of values? For a while it seemed that Phillips might have been correct, when during the televised Iran-Contra hearings Colonel Oliver North deflected congressional criticism of his behavior by turning his controlled anger on Congress and the media. For a time it seemed to strike a responsive chord with a segment of the American public. Nevertheless, his actions appeared to have only a transitory effect. The basic values expressed in honesty and integrity quickly consigned his performance to just that—an effective performance.

What seems to be at odds with Phillips's theory is the reliance on traditional forms of expression, traditional descriptions of role-playing and the like. Because most of our popular television shows are rich in cultural traditionalism, it is difficult to perceive Dr. Cliff Huxtable calling for a strong man on horseback to lead the nation. It is inconceivable to imagine the doctors of St. Elegis calling for the dissolution of Congress and its replacement by a rubber-stamp cabinet. One can hardly picture Slap Maxwell calling for a change in the Constitution, so that a president could remain in office for life. Maxwell would rather dwell on Enos Slaughter being elected to the Baseball Hall of Fame, or quoting Ernie Banks, "It's a beautiful day, let's play two."

As much as it is maligned for its "homogenized" programming, television may have actually served as a steadying influence, a reinforcing influence, as deterrent against large-scale outbreaks of extremism in this country. The nature of this beast has reaffirmed what makes us comfortable and well adjusted—and in the middle of the road.

Broadcasting the News and the Public: The Great Ambivalence

There appear to be contradictions in the public response to the "press." At the same time that the press is maligned by the public for reporting what some do not want to hear—or for being insensitive in times of tragedy or too hard on elected officials—that same public turns reporters into news celebrities themselves, stars in their own right. First it is who you watch, and only then the content that counts, and this can become a two-edged sword.

The antipress invective started with politicians during the Vietnam War, who blamed the press—mostly television news—for the public's dissatisfaction with the war. And like other aspects of that time, such as the generals, the press conferences held in Saigon, the images of burning and killing, this had a ring of truth. Who else could the politicians blame at that time except the press, especially television? The temptation remains to kill the messenger when the message is unwelcome.

Who can forget Vice President Spiro Agnew taking to the stump and deriding the media day after day in response to the burgeoning Watergate scandal? After the administration retreated in defeat after Watergate, the press staged a comeback and every young kid who could put two paragraphs together wanted to be an investigative reporter. That feeling did not last long, however, and reporters seem to have dropped on the popularity scale to a place somewhere between politicians and used-car salespeople. Perhaps it is best to recognize that, like other public enterprises that hold public awareness, confidence is not a fixed commodity, but rises and falls with the service performed at different events in different times.

How did television news react to their critics? ABC, for example, created a regularly scheduled program called "Viewpoint," which assessed the role of the media and allowed for debate on controversial issues. Its weeknight program "Nightline" also schedules controversial subjects, some of which have clear implications for the press.

If, as its critics decry, television uses politicians and reduces them to ashes, so do public figures use television to lambaste the press. Public figures use the press to criticize the press. The situation can become give and take on a grand scale. Ask any of those running for the position of presidential nominee of his party! This is give and take on a grand scale, public interest at its exciting best—rough, not always perfect, but vital and dynamic. As a result, the public is informed, sometimes excited, and democracy is served.

Interestingly enough, television drama and its predecessor, radio drama, have never really been good at their own public relations or image building. In radio days the early heroes were crusading newspapermen such as Steve Wilson of the *Illustrated Press* in Big Town, or the Green Hornet's real-life person Britt Reid, who ran the *Daily Sentinel* when he wasn't giving crooks a taste of his gas gun. No radio reporters here.

Television poked fun at its own and radio on "WKRP" and the "Mary Tyler Moore Show." Both were highly successful, but both pictured broadcasters as rather far out or inept but sweet characters. But when Mary Tyler Moore's Lou Grant switched from TV news director to editor of a newspaper, he became a heroic figure, something he was not in his Lou Grant role on MTM.

So television, and radio before it, never tried to create a good image of its news service through the vehicle of entertainment. Perhaps nobody has ever thought about it before. Or perhaps it is just not in the public interest to mix the two.

Some Introductory Thoughts

What you will read in the coming pages is not intended to be esoteric or high blown. These articles, for the most part, describe the products of day-to-day efforts by those who work in broadcasting and with broadcasters. They are serious, sometimes humorous, always related directly to the way the authors earn their livelihood. Their perceptions of public interest are governed by the response of their clients, their communities, and of those whose task it is to give legal meaning to the term. Public interest may be a vague term, but it is pervasive in broadcasting and comes with a history of specific examples.

Notes

1. Glendon Schubert, *The Public Interest: A Critique of the Theory of a Political Concept* (Glencoe, Ill.: The Free Press of Glencoe, 1960), 233.
2. Benjamin Barber, "The Second American Revolution," *Channels*, vol. 1, no. 6 (February/March 1982), 21.
3. Ibid., 22.
4. Ibid.
5. Ibid.
6. Ibid.

7. William A. Henry, III, "How Sweet It Still Is," *Channels of Communications*, vol. 5, no. 1 (May/June 1985), 57.

8. Kevin Phillips, *Post Conservative America* (New York: Random House, 1983), 195–96.

THE BROAD VIEW

1

AN IMPROVING WASTELAND

Perhaps the most familiar expression among reform-minded crusaders was created some twenty-five years ago by the then chairman of the Federal Communications Commission, Newton Minow. That expression was "vast wasteland." As with most emotionally loaded labels, the term "vast wasteland" has been used loosely as a general indictment of the broadcast industry, sometimes obscuring real issues in television programming.

In reflecting recently on what has happened since his first utterance of that expression, Newton Minow points to advancing technology and some specific programming to illustrate that there have been instances of improvement. He also notes, however, that broadcasters still have a way to go in order to fulfill more effectively their obligation to operate in the "public interest."

While Minow clearly expresses his concern over the broadcasters' treatment of the viewing audience, it is worth noting that this comes from an after-the-fact perspective. His concerns are programs already aired. He does not advocate taking any programs off the air. And that is how it should be. No action can be taken by the FCC or any other governmental body to restrain a licensee from airing a program. However, the broadcaster is held accountable at license renewal time for establishing a record of service in the public interest.

About the Author

Newton N. Minow is a partner in the firm of Sidley & Austin, Chicago. He was graduated with a B.S. degree from Northwestern

University in 1949 with majors in speech and political science. In 1950 he received his LL.B. degree from the Northwestern University School of Law, where he was editor-in-chief of the *Illinois Law Review*.

Minow was a law clerk to Supreme Court Chief Justice Fred M. Vinson from 1951 to 1952, administrative assistant to Illinois Governor Adlai E. Stevenson in 1952 to 1953, and special assistant to Stevenson during his presidential campaign in 1952.

In 1961 he was appointed chairman of the Federal Communications Commission by President John F. Kennedy and served in that position until 1963. During this appointment he gave his most famous speech. In an address to the National Association of Broadcasters on May 9, 1961, he invited his audience to spend a day in front of a television set and watch the "Vast Wasteland."

Newton Minow has been a professional lecturer at Northwestern University Medill School of Journalism and has authored books on broadcasting: *Equal Time: The Private Broadcaster and the Public Interest* (1966), and *Presidential Television* (1973), and *Tomorrow's American: Electronics and the Future* (1977) (co-author). He has served on many civic and corporate boards, including the Museum of Broadcast Communications in Chicago. He was the recipient of the George Foster Peabody Broadcasting Award in 1961.

TV's Still a "Vast Wasteland"—But Improving

NEWTON N. MINOW

On May 9, 1961, I stood nervously before the members of the National Association of Broadcasters to make my first speech as chairman of the Federal Communications Commission. I knew they would be dismayed by what I had to say, for these were words they had never heard from the FCC before. I would tell them they owed the American television viewers more public service than they were providing, and that we intended to make sure they took their responsibility seriously. I promised that, when the stations' licenses came to us for renewal, we would consider their commitment to the public interest in making our decisions.

I gave the broadcasters a long list of what I thought was right and wrong with television, and what our plans were to develop such experimental alternatives as pay-TV, UHF, and what we then called "educational television." But there are only two words among the thousands of words in that speech that people remember: "vast wasteland."

Those two words endured because viewers, then and now, too often feel stranded in a wasteland when they watch television, with oases of nourishment for the mind and spirit too far apart. Those two words about television still persist, despite momentous changes that were beyond my greatest hopes and fears back in 1961.

I see three changes as being the most significant.

The greatest single change over the last 25 years is the wider range of choice. In addition to public television, most people now have many more channels available through UHF, cable or satellite. And in even more profound a change, viewers with videocassette recorders can now watch TV programs when they want to see them. They can even watch prerecorded cassettes at their convenience. Outstanding television programs that were otherwise unavailable will now be cherished like the classics they are. While additional choices are not as diverse and high in quality as we still think they should be, the very fact of choice creates additional competition, which will impel producers in that direction.

Second, "educational television" in 1961 consisted too often of gray professors giving gray lectures before gray blackboards. Even that was unavailable in many communities, including the Nation's own capital. One of my proudest moments at the FCC was signing the license for WETA, the Greater Washington Educational Television Association. Now, my daughter Nell serves as a trustee of WETA, and my grandchildren are in love with *Sesame Street*. Public television enriches us with such programs as *American Playhouse*, *Great Performances*, *Live from Lincoln Center*, and *Nova*. Under the auspices of the Annenberg CPB Project, millions of viewers now can obtain college credit for course work centered on programs broadcast on public television. Although American public television has come far, I'm deeply disappointed by our failure to provide adequate funding. While Japan spent $10.09 per person on public television in 1983, we spent $3.02 that year. Of the more than 99 million individuals who watch public television weekly in the U.S., only 3.8 million subscribers contribute to it, a sad abdication of responsibility.

The third major change is in the coverage of news, which has improved dramatically since I called television a vast wasteland. Network news was then 15 minutes a night; it is now double that. Programs like *Nightline*, *The MacNeil/Lehrer NewsHour*, and the morning news programs amplify and illuminate the news. My own favorite, *CBS News Sunday Morning*, also inspires and uplifts the heart. A cable channel is now devoted entirely to news and another to coverage of Congress. We now have prime-time, network news programs like *20/ 20* and *60 Minutes*. All of this is a marvelous improvement. But it is not enough.

Television's greatest failure is in its role as an arena, a forum of candidates. Broadcasters spend millions of dollars and hundreds of hours to provide computer graphics to demonstrate the returns from every precinct. They use hundreds of hours of air time with commentary and analysis, but they spend little time simply turning the cameras on the candidates and allowing the candidates to explain their views. If I could make just one change in television today, it would be to provide candidates free air time for live presentations, either alone or in debates, to let viewers make decisions based on the best possible information.

Is television still a vast wasteland? I think the answer is a qualified yes. Vast? Certainly, and vaster by several orders of magnitude than it was 25 years ago. A wasteland? Yes, in the sense of wasted opportunities, though the oases are hearteningly lush and prospects look good for continued growth. Generally, prime-time entertainment shows are better than they were 25 years ago, but still tend to underestimate the intelligence of the viewer. The ultimate challenge is not to the Government or the networks but to the viewers. If television is not up to the standards you want for yourself and your family, there are things you can do. You can read a book, contribute to public television, rent a cassette, visit a friend—or even talk to your loved ones.

There are two words other than "vast wasteland" in that 25-year-old speech about television that I hope will survive 25 years from now. Those two words should always be linked with television: public interest.

2

PUBLIC INTEREST TRANSFORMED

This chapter places into an historical perspective the evolution of the legal perception of public interest. Although its original model cast the broadcaster in the role of trustee, the contemporary public interest concept is taking on a marketplace approach, more clearly in line with fuller and freer expression under the protection of the First Amendment.

In the following analysis, FCC and court decisions are shown to play a fundamental role in determining this important evolution. Careful attention is paid to the legislative activity as well, and using the fairness doctrine as a cornerstone in this careful analysis, the authors suggest that the future may lead to less intervention in programming by the government or FCC. However, the issues have yet to be finally resolved and the arguments, depending on their source, tend to reflect a muddled approach.

Perhaps what becomes most apparent in the ensuing account is that this country experiences difficulty in regulating information for whatever reason. This applies not only to broadcasting, but to other informational activities on both a national and international scale. Consider, for example, the information management problems created by the 1959 U–2 affair, or the recent Iran-Contra scandal. It is difficult to regulate information, even in the name of fairness or public interest, and still abide by the principles of the First Amendment. That is the way it should be.

About the Authors

Richard R. Zaragoza was born in Worcester, Massachusetts, on April 3, 1944 and admitted to the bar in 1969 in Massachusetts, and in 1970 in the District of Columbia. He received his A.B. from Georgetown University in 1966 and his J.D. from Boston College in 1969. He has served as an attorney for the Broadcast Bureau of the Federal Communications Commission (1969–1970) and the office of the general counsel, Appellate Litigation Division in Washington, D.C. (1970–1972). He is a member of the District of Columbia Bar, American and Federal Communications Bar Associations, where he has served as co-chairman of the Continuing Legal Education Committee (1979–1981), chairman of the Committee on Cooperation with Review Board and Administrative Law Judges (1981–1982), assistant secretary (1982–1983), secretary (1983–1984), member of the Executive Committee (1984–1987), and president elect 1988–present.

Richard J. Bodorff was born in Rockford, Illinois, on February 25, 1949 and was admitted to bar in 1974 in Tennessee and in 1975 in the District of Columbia. He received his B.A. cumlaude from Denison University in 1971, and his J.D. from Vanderbilt University in 1974. He has served as an attorney for the Legislation Division (1974–1976) and the Litigation Division (1976–1977) of the Office of General Counsel of the Federal Communications Commission in Washington, D.C. He was a member of the Board of Trustees of Denison University from 1977–1983 and has been a member of the Board of Directors of Central Virginia Educational Television Corporation since 1985. He is a member of the District of Columbia Bar and the Federal Communications Bar Associations.

Jonathan W. Emord was born in Brockton, Massachusetts, on January 16, 1961, and was admitted to the bar in 1985 in Illinois and in 1987 in the District of Columbia. He received a B.A. from the University of Illinois in 1982 and a J.D. from DePaul University in 1985. He was elected to Pi Sigma Alpha and was a James Scholar. He has served as an attorney for the Mass Media Bureau (1985–1986) of the Federal Communications Commission in Washington, D.C. He is a member of the First Amendment Task Force of the Center for Applied Jurisprudence as well as the District of Columbia Bar, the Illinois State Bar, the Federal Communications Bar, and the American Bar Associations. In the latter, he serves on the Forum Committee on Communications Law.

The Public Interest Concept Transformed: The Trusteeship Model Gives Way to a Marketplace Approach

RICHARD R. ZARAGOZA, RICHARD J. BODORFF, AND JONATHAN W. EMORD

In 1929, Congress enacted the Federal Radio Act.[1] For the first time in American history an entire press medium was made subject to federal government regulation.[2] By 1927, following the imposition of judicial limitations on the Commerce Department's licensing and channel allocation authority,[3] so many stations entered the radio marketplace that the federal government was not able to prevent a cacophonous collision of voices on the airwaves.[4] Between July 1926 and February 1927, nearly 200 new broadcasting stations came into existence, creating a total of 733.[5] With these stations operating on random, largely unregulated frequencies and employing fluctuating powers came frequent interference wars. Radio anarchy with a "babble of overlapping voices" was the result.[6]

On December 7, 1926, President Calvin Coolidge responded to the crisis, demanding that federal regulatory restraints be imposed upon radio. He stated:

> the authority of the department [of Commerce] under the law of 1912 has broken down; many more stations have been operating

Richard R. Zaragoza and Richard J. Bodorff are partners in the firm of Fisher, Wayland, Cooper and Leader in Washington, D.C. Jonathan W. Emord is an associate in that firm. All three are former Federal Communications Commission attorneys. The authors express their gratitude to Dan J. Sherman and Scott R. Flick for research assistance in the preparation of this chapter. The views expressed here are entirely those of the authors and do not represent the views of Fisher, Wayland, Cooper and Leader or other attorneys in its employment.

than can be accommodated within the limited number of wave-lengths available; ... many stations have departed from the scheme of allocation set down by the department, and ... this most important function has drifted into such chaos as seems likely, if not remedied, to destroy its great value.[7]

From the start, those intimately involved in creating the Radio Act found it necessary to characterize the airwaves as a public medium. Individuals "privileged" to use the medium were said to be vested with a "public trust," and the government's regulatory mandate over the airwaves was said to be in service to the "public interest."[8] That broadcasters be regulated and that broadcast licenses be issued to further the "public interest, convenience and necessity" was the foundation for regulation under the former Radio Act of 1927[9] and remains the mainstay for regulation under the Communications Act of 1934.[10] However, any apparent abiding consistency between 1934 and the present as a result of an unchanged "public interest" standard belies the fact that the "public interest" has always been an amorphous concept, serving as a basis both for constructing a regulatory labyrinth over the communications industry and, in recent years, for dismantling that labyrinth.

The Trusteeship Model

Until 1981, the predominant theory of broadcast regulation was the Trusteeship Model.[11] The underpinnings of FCC regulation rest in its foundation. Based upon this foundation, the FCC has been able to separate broadcasting from other industries[12] and impose upon it regulations that affect technical operating standards and, despite the industry's inextricable First Amendment nature, programming.[13] In awarding an applicant a license to operate a broadcast facility, the FCC historically has "not given a frequency solely for [the applicant's] ... own private purposes but ... in return for the grant ... [requires the applicant] to serve the public interest."[14] It has been the continuing duty of the FCC to assess a licensee's "performance and determine, on some rational basis, whether [licensee] program service has indeed been in the public interest."[15] When that performance has not met with FCC approval, the commission "has decided that the public interest would be better served by licensing someone else."[16]

Because the nature of broadcasting is communication, inevitable FCC attempts to gauge licensees "performance" have placed it in the role of assessing the merit of program content. Averse to that role of censorship due to First Amendment barriers to content-based regulation,[17] the FCC has found itself repeatedly caught in the midst of a dilemma: trying to assess licensee responsiveness to community needs without appearing to judge directly the worth of broadcast content.

The FCC's first major effort to influence program content came in 1946 with its release of the so-called "Blue Book," entitled *Public Service Responsibility of Broadcast Licensees*, in which the commission sought to require "balanced program fare."[18] Although never directly enforced, the Blue Book became an unofficial renewal standard to which broadcasters, at the urging of the commission, continuously adhered in an effort to secure license renewal.[19] Blue Book programming suggestions fell into four categories that were said to be given "particular consideration" by the commission in assessing whether broadcasters were fulfilling their public interest duties: (1) local and network programming carried on a sustaining (that is, noncommercial) basis, (2) local live programming, (3) programming devoted to discussion of public issues, and (4) hourly advertising.[20] In 1949 the commission supplemented this listing with the "fairness doctrine," obligating licensees to broadcast controversial issues of public importance and to air contrasting views on those issues.[21]

In 1960 the FCC extended its influence over program content review with its Report and Statement of Policy in the *En Banc Programming Inquiry*.[22] The Report and Statement emphasized that licensees were obliged to engage in "a diligent, positive and continuing effort ... to discover and fulfill the tastes and desires of [their] service area[s]."[23] As before, by abiding by commission program directives, a licensee otherwise in compliance with commission rules, would, at renewal time, likely be found to have "met his public responsibility."[24] Fourteen programming elements were urged as the *sine qua non* of service in the public interest.[25] A system of "ascertainment" was imposed upon licensees to insure that they incorporated these elements into their programming.[26] The commission imposed upon broadcasters a duty to cover issues of local interest and to originate a certain amount of that programming locally.[27] FCC "primers" were issued to inform licensees of proper methods of ascertaining community needs and interests.[28] These primers encouraged licensee canvassing of general public and community leader opinions.[29] Additionally, the commission set guidelines to preclude "over commercialization."[30] Network affiliates in the top fifty markets were required not to broadcast network or off-network programming from 7:00 to 8:00 P.M. Eastern Standard Time with exceptions for documentaries or children's programming.[31] This requirement, the so-called "prime time access rule," was designed to stimulate locally directed programming and provide an incentive for independent program producers. All broadcast stations were required to keep detailed program logs from sign-on to sign-off.[32] The commission's authority to impose such content related regulations was upheld in *NBC v. United States*[33] and its progeny.[34]

In effect, these regulations encouraged broadcasters to abide by programming norms favored by the FCC. In particular, licensees' programming promises were, at renewal time, scrutinized by the commission to assess if performance comported with them.[35]

The Trusteeship Model first began to unravel under the direction of former FCC Chairman Charles D. Ferris. However, in 1981, under former FCC Chairman Mark S. Fowler, deregulation became a paramount FCC policy objective. Since then, a different concept of the "public interest" has become predominant in commission regulatory policy: A Marketplace Approach to broadcasting.[36]

The Marketplace Approach

Under the Marketplace Approach, licensees are not viewed as holding a public trust in exchange for which they must perform certain prescribed duties. Rather, they are "marketplace participants."[37] Under this approach "market forces rather than [FCC] judgments on program service . . . determine where the public interest lies in broadcasting."[38] While under the Trusteeship Model, the right of the public to be informed is paramount,[39] under the Marketplace Approach, the right of the broadcaster to speak predominates.[40] In the case of the former, the broadcast medium is part of the public domain; in the case of the latter, this is not necessarily so.[41] Moreover, whereas the Trusteeship Model presumes scarcity of spectrum space,[42] the Marketplace Approach finds scarcity both irrelevant to First Amendment analysis[43] and, in fact, nonexistent.[44] The Marketplace Approach, therefore, seeks full First Amendment protection for the broadcast media.[45]

The Marketplace Approach is premised upon the view that to profit, entrepreneurs must provide to consumers goods of value and utility. In doing so, each entrepreneur is led toward maximal fulfillment of societal needs. He is "led by an invisible hand to promote an end which was no part of his intention"[46] but which, in the course of "pursuing this own interest[.] . . . frequently promotes that of the society more effectually than when he really intends to promote it."[47] The Marketplace Approach incorporates the view that commission regulatory policies that award and renew licenses to those who fulfill certain content guidelines deny the American consumer maximum satisfaction from the medium by interfering with the broadcasters' direct fulfillment of consumer demand.[48]

Moreover, the Marketplace Approach incorporates the view that the Trusteeship Model licensee selection process—based on legal preferences which favor local owners, owners with the smallest number of other media interests, minority and female owners, and owners with extensive past broadcast and local civic experience[49]—disserves the public interest by preventing the economic resource at stake, the spectrum, from reaching its "best and highest use."[50] In market theory, the best and highest use of a resource can only be attained when that resource is employed by an entrepreneur who has, through competition, established an economically superior claim to the resource.[51] According to many marketplace theorists, to attain the best and highest use, the spectrum must be auctioned to the highest bidder.[52]

Some adherents of the Marketplace Approach favor withdrawing all allocated spectrum from licensed users for subsequent government resale to the highest bidder.[53] Thereafter, the spectrum would be a private-property interest capable of resale without interference from government.

Other adherents of the Marketplace Approach, including former FCC Chairman Mark S. Fowler, favor granting existing licensee's "squatter's rights" to their frequencies.[54] Thereafter, each licensee could resell its spectrum without government approval to new non-licensee highest bidders, who would thereby make best and highest use of the resource. Newly adopted spectrum would, however, be subject to direct auction, for its sale would not entail disruption of service to the public.

Consistent with the Marketplace Approach, the FCC since 1981 has engaged in extensive deregulatory efforts, much of which have been designed to relieve broadcasters of former programming obligations. The commission abolished its ascertainment requirements and its percentage guidelines for news and public affairs programming,[55] its programming guidelines for television and its promise versus performance standard of renewal reviews,[56] its program log requirements,[57] and its guidelines to preclude over commercialization.[58] Perhaps most significantly, the commission recently ended enforcement of the fairness doctrine.[59]

The fairness doctrine had stood for over thirty-seven years as the central pillar in support of the Trusteeship Model.[60] The fairness doctrine was deemed constitutional by the Supreme Court in *Red Lion Broadcasting Co. v. FCC* premised upon an alleged scarcity of broadcast spectrum. This scarcity of spectrum is the same scarcity that forms a primary basis for broadcast regulation generally. Therefore, if it can be proven that no scarcity exists or that spectrum scarcity is an illegitimate basis for regulation, it is conceivable that the FCC regulatory apparatus will have to be further reduced. Moreover, it is possible that spectrum auctions now a part of Marketplace Approach theory will be formally introduced. Consequently, the struggle leading to the elimination of the fairness doctrine is revealing of the future directions that the public interest concept may take as the FCC continues to develop its Marketplace Approach.

The Demise of the Fairness Doctrine: A Study in the Public Interest[61]

In 1949, the commission formally adopted the fairness doctrine.[62] It has ever since been the source of vigorous,[63] at times vituperative,[64] debate. In the midst of this debate and in the face of intense congressional opposition,[65] the commission under the chairmanship of Dennis R. Patrick ended enforcement of the doctrine on August 6, 1987.[66] It did so following President Ronald Reagan's June 19, 1987, veto[67] of a congressional attempt to codify the doctrine[68] and a strong indication by the President that he would continue to veto any bill to which the doctrine may be attached.[69]

From its inception, the doctrine had imposed upon broadcasters "certain obligations to afford reasonable opportunity for the discussion of conflicting views on issues of public importance."[70] In the year of its genesis, 1949, the fairness doctrine was deemed by the FCC to be inextricably a part of the Trusteeship Model for broadcasting.

In that year, the commission chose to subordinate the broadcaster's editorial discretion to its concept of the public interest, noting that the interests of the community were paramount.[71] The rationale hinged on the premise that "[i]t is [the] right of the public to be informed, rather than any right on the part of the Government, any broadcast licensee or any individual member of the public to broadcast his own particular views . . . which is the foundation stone of the American system of broadcasting."[72]

Finding that the public interest required that the public's right to know takes precedence over the broadcast editor's right to speak when the two rights came into conflict, the commission stated:

> Licensee editorialization is but one aspect of freedom of expression by means of radio. Only insofar as it is exercised in conformity with the paramount right of the public to hear a reasonably balanced presentation of all responsible viewpoints on particular issues can such editorialization be considered to be consistent with . . . the public interest.[73]

The FCC tied this construction of the public interest to the Trusteeship Model for broadcasting.

In 1959 Congress amended section 315(a) of the Communications Act of 1934[74] to read in pertinent part as follows:

Nothing in the foregoing sentence shall be construed as relieving broadcasters, in connection with the presentation of newscasts, news interviews, news documentaries and on-the-spot coverage of news events, from the obligation imposed upon them under this Act to operate in the public interest and *to afford reasonable opportunity for the discussion of conflicting views on issues of public importance.*[75]

In doing so, however, Congress did not appear to anticipate a question of interpretation that would trouble First Amendment lawyers and scholars for years to come: Did Congress intend to codify the fairness doctrine into the Communications Act of 1934, as amended, or merely retain the FCC's existing policy and therefore its discretion over the matter?

Proponents of the fairness doctrine have argued that the language codified the doctrine and mandated its enforcement.[76] Opponents have contended, to the contrary, that the language merely acknowledged the existence of commission fairness doctrine policy, but did not mandate that policy.[77] The House and Senate discussions of the amendment include no unequivocal indication of the intended purpose.

Unclear Legislative History

Senator William Proxmire (D-Wis) offered the original version of the amendment in the Senate.[78] No House member offered a similar amendment. Proxmire, at the time, stated that the amendment "merely expresses the philosophy that the media of radio and television are in the public domain, and that they must render, under the law, public service, and that wherever it is practical and possible the situation must bring to light all sides of a controversy in the public interest."[79]

Subsequent debate has centered on whether Proxmire intended to codify the fairness doctrine in Sec. 315(a) or simply to acknowledge the FCC's power to enforce its policy. Subsequently, Proxmire stated that, at the time, he did intend to codify the doctrine.[80] The Senate committee report referencing the amendment, however, provides that "the committee does not diminish or affect in any way Federal Communications Commission policy or existing law."[81]

The joint conference committee altered, without explanation, the language of the Proxmire amendment to its present form, although the essential meaning of the amendment was said to have been preserved.[82] The post-conference debates do not show that Congress focused on whether this amendment was in fact an effort to codify the fairness doctrine.[83] This ambiguity made it incumbent upon the Supreme Court to determine the operative meaning of Sec. 315(a). When afforded the opportunity to do so in the 1969 *Red Lion* case, the Court did not definitely resolve the issue.

Enter Red Lion

In its *Red Lion* decision, the Supreme Court rejected a First Amendment challenge to the validity of the fairness doctrine and of related rules concerning licensee broadcast of personal attacks and political editorials. The Court determined that the doctrine "finds specific recognition in statutory form, is in part modeled on explicit statutory provisions relating to political candidates, and is approvingly reflected in legislative history,"[84] "[I]n adopting the new regulations," reasoned the Court, "the Commission was implementing congressional policy rather than embarking on a frolic of its own."[85]

The Court accepted the rationale articulated by the FCC in its 1949 report, explaining that "[i]t is the right of the viewers and listeners, not the right of the broadcasters, which is paramount."[86] This rationale for regulation is in stark contrast to the print media, where it is argued that the right of the editor is paramount to that of the public.[87]

In searching for a factual basis on which to distinguish the broadcast from the print media and afford the former lessened First Amendment protection, the Court adopted the notion that the broadcast spectrum was scarce and therefore uniquely appropriate for government regulation. "Where there are substantially more individuals who want to broadcast than there are frequencies to allocate," reasoned the Court, "it is idle to posit an unabridgeable First Amendment right of every individual to speak, write or publish."[88]

Despite the apparent certainty of its holding, the *Red Lion* Court did not resolve the issue of whether Congress in 1959 had intended to codify the fairness doctrine into the Communications Act of 1934, as amended. Moreover, it expressed a future basis for reexamination of the holding. The *Red Lion* Court submitted in dicta that "if experience" ordained that "the net effect of [administration of the doctrine was to reduce] rather than [enhance] the volume and quality of coverage, there will be time enough to reconsider the constitutional implications."[89] Moreover, the Court premised its scarcity of broadcast spectrum rationale upon an inherently dated record: "the present state of commercially acceptable technology as of 1969."[90]

The Red Lion decision has been studied methodically by those who have sought to retain as well as those who have succeeded in ending enforcement of the fairness doctrine. On the question of codification, although the Court did strongly suggest that the doctrine was "in part modeled on explicit statutory provision ... [and] reflected in legislative history,"[91] it did also state, in an apparently contradictory fashion, that the "statutory authority" to promulgate the doctrine is derived from Section 303 of the Communications Act, which provides a plenary grant of congressional power to the FCC to regulate as the "public convenience, interest, or necessity requires."[92]

In 1974, in the face of renewed questioning of the doctrine's validity and efficacy, the FCC evaluated the fairness doctrine's twenty-five-year history.[93] Based on this evaluation, it reiterated its strong commitment to the doctrine in light of the *Red Lion* decision.

Exit Red Lion

In July of 1984 the Supreme Court sent a carefully worded message in dicta to the FCC. That message indicated the high Court's apparent concern over the continued validity of spectrum scarcity as a rationale for broadcast regulation. In footnote 11 to *FCC v. League of Women Voters of Cal.*,[94] the Court stated:

> The prevailing rationale for broadcast regulation based on spectrum scarcity has come under increasing criticism in recent years. Critics, including the incumbent Chairman of the FCC, charge that with the advent of cable and satellite television technology, communities now have access to such a wide variety of stations that the scarcity doctrine is obsolete.... *We are not prepared, however, to reconsider our long-standing approach without some signal from Congress or the FCC that technological developments have advanced so far that some revision of broadcast regulation may be required.*[95]

In August 1985 the FCC acted on the Court's suggestion. In a dramatic policy reversal, the Commission rejected the public interest basis for the doctrine but fell short of eliminating it because of its concern that Congress had not granted authority to do so.[96]

Consistent with the burgeoning Marketplace Approach to broadcast regulation, the FCC embraced the view that a multiplicity of new technologies unknown to the marketplace of 1969 rendered spectrum scarcity an outdated rationale.[97] Indeed, the commission now found the public interest disserved by the fairness doctrine, stating:

> We no longer believe that the Fairness Doctrine, as a matter of policy, serves the public interest. We believe that the interest of the public in viewpoint diversity is fully served by the multiplicity of voices in the marketplace today and that the intrusion by government into the content of programming occasioned by the enforcement of the

doctrine necessarily restricts the journalistic freedom of broadcasters.[98]

The FCC also determined that the doctrine "actually [inhibited] the
presentation of controversial issues of public importance: by causing
broadcasters to avoid coverage of those issues in order to eliminate
the possibility of having to defend against fairness doctrine complaints."[99] This "chilling" effect on speech, explained the commission,
is a detriment to the public and "in degradation of the editorial
prerogatives of broadcast journalists."[100]

Although convinced that the spectrum scarcity rationale was ob-
solete and that enforcement of the fairness doctrine ran contrary to
the public interest, the commission fell short of abolishing it, choosing
instead to await congressional action.[101] The FCC had no clear authority from either Congress or the courts to abolish the doctrine
until the D.C. Circuit Court's decision in *Meredith Corp. v. F.C.C.*[102]

Bork Takes a Step

Just before *Meredith*, in *Telecommunications Research & Action Center v. F.C.C.*,[103] D.C. Circuit Judge Robert H. Bork[104] expressed in dicta
grounds for the repudiation of the spectrum scarcity rationale.[105] In
upholding the FCC's decision not to apply the fairness doctrine to
teletext,[106] Judge Bork stated that reliance upon spectrum scarcity
as a rationale for imposing government regulation upon the broadcast
and not the print media created a distinction without a genuine difference.[107]

> It is certainly true that broadcast frequencies are scarce but it is
> unclear why that fact justifies content regulation of broadcasting in
> a way that would be intolerable if applied to the editorial process
> of the print media. All economic goods are scarce, not least the
> newsprint, ink delivery trucks, computers, and other resources that
> go into the production and dissemination of print journalism. Not
> everyone who wishes to publish a newspaper, or even a pamphlet,
> may do so. Since scarcity is a universal fact, it can hardly explain
> regulation in one context and not another.[108]

Bork stated that the fairness doctrine was not specifically mandated
by Congress and thus was subject to FCC "public interest" redeter-
mination. The Supreme Court has let the decision in *Telecommunications Research & Action Center* stand.[109]

The commission initially sought to leave to Congress the question
of the doctrine's constitutionality. It was not until the D.C. Circuit's
remand in *Meredith Corp.* that the FCC elected to act.[110]

The Meredith Case

In the summer of 1982, Meredith Corporation's station WTVH in Syracuse, New York, broadcast three advertisements sponsored by the Energy Association of New York. The Syracuse Peace Council (SPC) challenged these advertisements as violating the fairness doctrine because the advertisements promoted the Nine Mile II nuclear power plant "as a sound investment for New York's future" without presenting opposing viewpoints.[111]

The FCC found on December 20, 1984, that Meredith had violated the fairness doctrine, concluding that the advertisements raised a controversial issue of public importance concerning the economic soundness of the plant, and thus that Meredith had acted unreasonably in failing to present viewpoints opposed to the plant.[112] The commission ordered Meredith to explain how it would comply with its fairness doctrine obligations.[113]

Meredith filed a petition for reconsideration, arguing that the FCC erred in applying the fairness doctrine. Meredith argued that it had acted reasonably by subsequently offering the SPC a chance to air its own ads.[114] After the petition for reconsideration period lapsed, Meredith moved to file a supplemental pleading in which it contended that the fairness doctrine was unconstitutional.

While the petition was pending, the commission issued its 1985 *Fairness Report.* In light of its decision to enforce the doctrine while awaiting congressional action, the FCC denied Meredith's petition.[115] This was the first determination of its kind by the commission in five years. Meredith then sought review in the D.C. Circuit Court, alleging that the commission had arbitrarily and capriciously enforced the doctrine and that the doctrine contravened the First Amendment.[116]

In its decision, the D.C. Circuit agreed that the FCC had correctly followed precedent in choosing to apply the doctrine,[117] but held that the commission had acted unlawfully in refusing to consider Meredith's constitutional claim.[118] In pertinent part, the court faulted the FCC for not clarifying whether the fairness doctrine was mandated by statute or was "self-generated" pursuant to the commission's plenary "public interest" power.[119] The court stated that if the commission found the doctrine was not specifically codified by Congress, it could avoid the constitutional issue by declaring the doctrine contrary to the public interest on an adequate record.[120] The case was remanded to the FCC to address the constitutional issue.[121]

In response to the remand order, the commission took the extraordinary step of inviting public comment on whether "enforcement of the fairness doctrine is constitutional and whether enforcement of the doctrine is contrary to the public interest."[122] Six months later, the FCC vacated its judgment against Meredith Corporation and ended enforcement of the fairness doctrine.[123]

The commission determined "based upon ... our experience in administering the fairness doctrine, fundamental constitutional principles, and the findings contained in ... [the] 1985 Fairness Report ... [that the] doctrine, on its face, violates the First Amendment and contravenes the public interest."[124] Emboldened by the court's remand and by the President's June 19, 1987, veto[125] of a congressional bill to recodify the fairness doctrine,[126] the FCC acted unilaterally and, in doing so, pitted itself against Congress in a constitutional struggle. Appeals will ultimately place the issue of the doctrine's constitutionality before the Supreme Court, where the embroglio between the president, the FCC, and the D.C. Circuit Court of Appeals, on the one hand, and the Congress, on the other, can be definitively resolved.[127] The Court's decision will either create a new basis for continuation of the Trusteeship Model or will accelerate the full implementation of the Marketplace Approach.

Conclusion

As the Trusteeship Model has given way to the Marketplace Approach, fundamental changes have effected new relationships between the government and broadcasters and between broadcasters and the public. The Trustee concept long interwoven with the public interest has been disentangled from it by deregulation. Deregulation alone, however, did not produce the most remarkable change. Rather, the establishment of a new marketplace ideology in the FCC has transformed the public interest itself, and this change has been revolutionary.

Until this decade, FCC regulators had accepted the notion that broadcasting, perhaps more than any other industry, made use of a limited, intangible, and intrinsically public resource—the broadcast spectrum. They reasoned that this resource could not be rationally distributed by market forces and pointed to the cacophonous collision of voices on the airwaves in the late 1920s as the ultimate consequence of market allocation.

Through years of effort to discover a nonmarketplace means to distribute spectrum, FCC regulators settled upon a plethora of rules, each separately premised upon idealized value judgments favoring certain kinds of broadcast programming and behavior over others. The *sine qua non* of broadcasting in the public interest and of license renewal became proof of a broadcaster's adherence to these policy preferences, even to the exclusion of contrary editorial and marketplace judgments.

Beginning in earnest in the 1980s, the FCC shifted course dramatically and began laying siege to the Trusteeship citadel. The language of service in the public interest changed from goal-oriented "public interest" concepts to privately oriented marketplace concepts. Increasingly, the "public interest" was viewed as not what the government said it was but what the broadcaster found it to be, premised not upon the idealized conception of FCC regulators but upon the marketplace forces directing broadcasting.

The government now stands poised on a precipice of history. It must determine whether the public interest, no longer securely grounded in the Trusteeship Model, will be shifted in toto to rest in the Marketplace Approach or whether the Trusteeship Model will be revised to emerge in modified form. The ultimate outcome of this struggle is still an open question.

Many regulatory vestiges of the Trusteeship Model remain in place, and Congress appears to favor reimposition of others. Indeed some regulatory constructs like the "reasonable access" and "equal opportunity" rules (mandating the provision of unedited air time to legally qualified candidates) and the "meritorious" programming service renewal standard are thoroughly entrenched in FCC regulations and precedent because they reflect statutory standards. The majority in the Congress favors these regulations. The FCC, under Chairman Dennis Patrick's direction, opposes these regulations and favors further deregulation. Similarly, in the judiciary, the Supreme Court has hinted that it may be willing to eviscerate the spectrum scarcity rationale which supports *all* nontechnical FCC regulations, and the D.C. Circuit Court is on record, in dicta, as deeming illegitimate the spectrum scarcity rational.

Consequently, a major constitutional showdown is in the offing. Ultimately, the Supreme Court will have to determine whether the spectrum scarcity rationale and nontechnical regulations premised upon it are consistent with the First Amendment. The Court will also have to determine whether the Trusteeship Model can be justified by resort to other public-interest concepts that have constitutional support.

On the one hand, if the Court finds the spectrum scarcity rational inconsistent with the First Amendment, this could well create a constitutional bar to nontechnical regulation and would make possible the full implementation of the Marketplace Approach. On the other hand, if the Court finds a different rationale for regulation or relegitimizes the spectrum scarcity rationale, reregulation and the reinstitution of the Trusteeship Model would be possible.

Should the Supreme Court decide that spectrum scarcity is an illegitimate basis for regulation, the FCC may choose to replace the

Trusteeship Model with the Marketplace Approach. Inevitably, attention will then turn to the policy implications involved in the use of auctions for the allocation of broadcast spectrum.

According to market theorists, auctions would permit spectrum to be put to its "best and highest use," causing those with the greatest economic resources and desire to invest in broadcasting to supplant those who would otherwise be chosen under a system of policy preferences. Broadcasters would obtain property rights to use and enjoyment of the allocated spectrum conditioned upon maintenance of approved engineering parameters.

Before the FCC can act to implement any system, the Congress must amend the Communications Act to create a statutory basis for broadcast auctions. Several alternative auction systems are possible.

These systems would result in government sale of newly allocated spectrum to the highest bidders. Different proposals exist for currently allocated spectrum.[128] This latter spectrum could be priced at an appraised value. Each allocated and valued spectrum segment could then be offered to each respective licensee who operates on that spectrum under reasonable purchase terms. If, within a specified time, a licensee failed to purchase its spectrum, the spectrum could revert to the government for open market bidding, creating—in effect—a forced assignment. Alternatively, current spectrum could be leased by the government to existing licensees. Such leasing could be indefinite, with an option to purchase the spectrum at an appraised price. Alternatively, current spectrum could be leased to existing licensees for an indefinite period at a substantial discount rate below market levels in recognition of the licensee's years of good faith reliance upon the policy preference allocation system. Alternatively the leasing could be definite, with a requirement that spectrum be purchased by a certain future cut-off date. After the cut-off date, the commission could permit the spectrum to be assigned by the licensee within a certain time period to another who pledges a willingness to purchase it. If the licensee were unable to assign the spectrum to such a purchaser, it would revert to the government. An assignee under such a system would then have an obligation to continue lease payments to the government until a specified date at which time it would be required to purchase the spectrum outright from or permit the spectrum to revert to the government. If the spectrum were to revert to the government, the government could then auction it to the highest bidder.

Numerous other possibilities exist. The allocated spectrum could remain subject to government licensing until the first assignment. Thereupon, the government could assess an assignment fee from the assignor and the assignee at assignment filing time. Upon approval of the assignment, the government could (in exchange for the fee payment) issue to the assignee a conditional guarantee to indefinite use and enjoyment of the spectrum (conditioned upon proper maintenance of engineering parameters).

Long-term results of an auction system are difficult to predict. Some contend that auctions will cause spectrum to go to the best-financed but not necessarily the most experienced and capable broadcasters. Others contend that the highest bidder, by definition, would be the most experienced, best financed, and most efficient. If this latter type of bidder predominates in practice, the current system of market protectionism would be replaced by a more directly competitive broadcast market. Licensees are now shielded from competition to a certain extent by the commission's policy preference spectrum allocation system. New licensees entering the market after a comparative hearing are not necessarily the most economically viable and marketwise competitors. Rather, they may be new, inexperienced owners whose proposals have satisfied commission policies, which tend to favor minority and/or female local residents who have no other broadcast interests and are active in their communities. An auction system will favor market entrants with substantial capital and with extensive business and/or broadcast ownership and experience. Programming to attract maximum audience (and, hence, advertisers) would be the primary, if not sole, objective. Full implementation of an auction system will therefore likely produce greater competition in local markets. Some have suggested that this competition will cause programming to be geared toward maximum mass market appeal, rendering it bland. Others believe that the degree and quality of innovative programming may well increase as broadcasters struggle to grab the attention of viewers.

The future of broadcast regulation has reached a critical juncture. Whether the auction system and the Marketplace Approach will replace the Trusteeship Model is now dependent upon resolution of the ideological and constitutional struggle being waged by the courts and the FCC, on the one hand, and the Congress, on the other. In the decade ahead, the outcome of this struggle will have a profound impact upon the way in which the broadcasting business is conducted in our society.

Notes

1. Ch. 169, 44 Stat. 1162, *repealed by* Communications Act of 1934, Ch. 652, Sec. 602 (a), 48 Stat. 1064, 1102. The Federal Radio Act of 1927 was preceded by the Radio Act of 1912, Ch. 287, 37 Stat. 302 (1912), *repealed by* Communications Act of 1934, Ch. 652, Sec. 602 (a), 48 Stat. 1064, 1102. The

1912 Act vested in the Secretary of Commerce and Labor limited power to require licenses for use of radio apparatuses. The act was designed to end the "etheric bedlam produced by numerous stations all trying to communicate at once" in ship-to-ship and ship-to-shore radio communications prior to its adoption. S. Rep. No. 659, 61 Cong., 2d Sess. 4 (1910).

2. The First Amendment to the Constitution of the United States reads in pertinent part: "Congress shall make no law ... abridging the freedom of speech, or of the press.... " In the 1789 framing of the First Amendment, James Madison stated that it was to mean "nothing more than this, that the people have a right to express and communicate their sentiments and wishes. ... [and that] the liberty of the press is expressly declared to be beyond the reach of this Government.... " *The Debates and Proceedings in the Congress of the United States* 766, 1st Cong., 1st Sess. (Washington, 1834). The conclusion that the freedoms of speech and press were beyond the intended powers of the federal government is confirmed by one of the foremost First Amendment legal historians, Leonard W. Levy:

> [The First Amendment] was intended and understood to prohibit any congressional regulation of the press, whether by means of censorship, a licensing law, a tax, or a sedition act. The Framers meant Congress to be totally without power to enact legislation respecting the press.

L. Levy, *Emergence of a Free Press* (New York: 1985), 269–270.

3. *See Hoover v. Intercity Radio Co.*, 286 F. 1003 (D.C. Cir. 1923), *appeal dismissed*, 266 U.S. 636 (1924); *United States v. Zenith Group*, 12 F.2d 614 (N.D. Ill. 1926).

4. In noting the disquieting degree of unanimity on the need for government regulation, Herbert Hoover stated in 1924 that he believed broadcasting "probably the only industry of the United States that is unanimously in favor of having itself regulated." *quoted in* G. Head, *Broadcasting in America: A survey of Television and Radio* 126 (3rd ed. 1976).

5. Herring and Gross, *Telecommunications* 224 (1936).

6. Nicholas Johnson, "Towers of Babel: the Chaos in Radio Spectrum Utilization and Allocation," 34 *Law & Contemporary Problems* 505 (1969); *see also* E. Barnouw, *Tower of Babel*, 31 (1966); *NBC v. United States*, 319 U.S. 190, 212 (1943) ("With everybody on the air, nobody could be heard").

7. Davis, *Law of Radio Communication* 54 (1927).

8. In Congressional hearings preceding adoption of the Radio Act of 1927, Herbert Hoover stated: "Radio communication is not to be considered as merely a business carried on for private gain, for private advertisement or for entertainment of the curious. It is a public concern impressed with the public trust and is to be considered primarily from the standpoint of public interest to the same extent and upon the basis of the general principles as our other public utilities." Hearings on H.R. 7357 Before the House Comm. on Merchant Marine & Fisheries, 68th Cong. 1st Sess. 10 (1924).

9. Radio Act of 1927, Ch. 169, 44 Stat. 1162 (1927).

10. 47 U.S.C. Subsec. 303, 307(a) (1984).

11. Early in radio regulatory history, the government defined the fun-

damental basis for this theory. In 1930, the Federal Radio Commission stated that:

> [despite the fact that] [t]he conscience and judgment of a station's management are necessarily personal, ... the station itself must be operated as if owned by the public. ... It is as if people of a community should own a station and turn it over to the best man in sight with this injunction: 'Manage this station in our interest'. ... The standing of every station is determined by that conception.

See "The Federal Radio Commission and the Public Service Responsibility of Broadcast Licensees," 11 Fed. Comm. B.J. 5, 14 (1950).

12. See *NBC v. United States*, 319 U.S. 190, 213 (1943), wherein it is stated that: "Unlike other modes of expression, radio inherently is not available to all. ... [This] is why, unlike other modes of expression, it is subject to government regulation."

13. Early in FCC history, the Supreme Court placed its imprimatur not only behind FCC technical regulation to guard against radio frequency interference but also behind FCC program regulation. In *NBC v. United States*, 319 U.S. 190 (1943), Justice Frankfurter stressed that the Communications Act of 1934 did not limit the FCC to being a "traffic officer, policing the wavelengths to prevent stations from interfering with each other ...," but also "upon the Commission the burden of determining the composition of that traffic." The FCC took "composition of that traffic" to mean programming responsive to community interests and needs. *See Report and Statement of Policy re: Commission En Banc Programming Inquiry*, 20 R.R. 1901 (1960).

Even before the *NBC* case in 1937, the commission had sought to expand its regulatory influence over licensee programming. In a speech before the National Conference on Educational Broadcasting on December 1, 1937, Commissioner Payne stated: "First, we must establish in practice what has been accepted in theory and law—that the radio waves are the inalienable property of the public. Program standards must be established corresponding to technical standards. The broadcaster should be required at regular intervals to account for his stewardship, and if he has not met the standards set, the frequency he enjoys should be thrown into the public domain and made available to those who can and will meet the program standards, for program standards are more important than technical standards."

14. Kenneth A. Cox, "'The FCC's Role in Television Programming Regulation," 14 *Villanova Law Review* 590, 592 (1969).

15. Ibid.

16. Ibid.

17. "If we advert to the nature of republican government," said James Madison to the House of Representatives, "we shall find that the censorial power is in the people over the government, and not in the government over the people." 4 *Annals of Congress* 934 (1794); *see also* 47 U.S.C. Sec. 326; *CBS v. DNC*, 412 U.S. 94 at 145–46 (1983), in which Justice Stewart, concurring, said: "If we must choose whether editorial decisions are to be made in the free judgment of individual broadcasters, or imposed by bureaucratic fiat, the choice must be for freedom." *Police Department of Chicago v. Moseley*,

408 U.S. 92, 95 (1972), in which the Court stated "[A]bove all else, the First Amendment means that government has no power to restrict expression because of its message, its ideas, its subject matter, or its content." Even where a challenged regulation restricts freedom of expression only incidentally, the Supreme Court will scrutinize the governmental interest furthered by the regulation and will declare it invalid if it is not narrowly tailored to serve a compelling state purpose. *See, e.g., Shad v. Borough of Mt. Ephraim,* 452 U.S. 16–69 (1981); *United States v. O'Brien,* 391 U.S. 367–377 (1967).

18. FCC, *Public Service Responsibility of Broadcast Licensees* (1946). For application, see *Eugene J. Roth (Mission Broadcasting Co.),* 12 F.C.C. 102 (1947); *Howard W. Davis,* 12 F.C.C. 91 (1947); *Community Broadcasting Co.,* 12 F.C.C. 85 (1947). The Commission discussed the Blue Book approach in *Deregulation of Radio,* 84 F.C.C. 2d 960, 994–95 (1981).

19. "The Commission proposed a quantitative evaluation of a station's overall performance. A half-dozen categories of programming were established.... So long as stations maintained a fair balance between the various categories, their renewals were automatic." Ben C. Fisher, "Program Control and the Federal Communications Commission: A Limited Role," 14 *Villanova Law Review* 602, 607 (1969).

20. See FCC, *Public Service Responsibility of Broadcast Licensees, supra,* at note 18.

21. *Report on Editorializing by Broadcast Licensees,* 13 F.C.C. 1246 (1949).

22. 44 F.C.C. 2303 (1960).

23. Ibid., at 2312.

24. Ibid.

25. Ibid., at 2314.

26. *See Ascertainment of Community Problems,* 57 F.C.C. 2d 418 (1976); 47 C.F.R. Sec. 73.4020 (1981).

27. *See* 47 C.F.R. Sec. 73.1120(b)(2)(1980).

28. *See, e.g., Primer on Ascertainment of Community Problems by Broadcast Applicants,* 27 F.C.C. 2d 650 (1973).

29. *See, e.g., Television Program Form,* 5 F.C.C. 2d 175 (1966); *Renewal of Broadcast Licenses,* 44 F.C.C. 2d 405 (1973); *Ascertainment of Community Programs by Broadcast Applicants,* 57 F.C.C. 2d 418 (1976); *Revision of FCC Form 303,* 54 F.C.C. 2d 750 (1976); 47 C.F.R. Sec. 0.281(a)(8) (1981); 47 C.F.R. Sec. 0.281(a)(8) (1981).

30. *See* 47 C.F.R. Sec. 73.4010 (1982).

31. *National Association of Independent Television Producers & Distributors v. FCC,* 516 F. 2d 526 (2d Cir. 1975).

32. 47 C.F.R. Sec. 73.1800; Sec. 73.1810; Sec. 73.1850 (1980).

33. *See NBC v. United States,* 319 U.S. 190 (1943).

34. *See, e.g. CBS v. FCC,* 453 U.S. 267 (1981); *National Association of Independent Television Producers & Distributors v. F.C.C.,* 516 F.2d 526 (2d Cir. 1975); *National Association of Independent Television Producers & Distributors v. F.C.C.,* 502 F.2d 249 (2d Cir. 1974); *Mt. Mansfield Television, Inc. v. F.C.C.,* 442 F.2d 470 (2d Cir. 1971); *see also, "Peculiar Characteristics": An Analysis of the First Amendment Implications of Broadcast Regulation,* 31 Fed. Comm. L.J. 1 (1978).

35. *See, e.g., KORD, Inc.*, 31 F.C.C. 85 (1961); *Moline Television Corp.*, 31 F.C.C. 2d 263 (1971); *Simon Geller*, 90 F.C.C. 2d 250 (1982).

36. "Put simply, I believe that we are at the end of regulating broadcasting under the trusteeship model. Whether you call it 'paternalism' or 'nannyism,' it is 'Big Brother,' and it must cease. I believe in a marketplace approach to broadcast regulation.... Under the coming marketplace approach, the Commission should, as far as possible, defer to a broadcaster's judgment about how best to compete for viewers and listeners, because this serves the public interest." Mark S. Fowler, "The Public Interest," *The Florida Bar Journal*, March 1982.

37. Fowler & Brenner, *A Marketplace Approach to Broadcast Regulation*, 60 Tex. L. Rev. 207, 209 (1982).

38. Ibid., at 233.

39. *See Red Lion Broadcasting Co., v. FCC*, 395 U.S. 367, 390 (1969) ("It is the right of the viewers and listeners, not the right of the broadcasters, which is paramount.")

40. "First, it should be noted that the language of the first amendment protects the right of speech, not the right of access to ideas or even the right to listen. The direct concern of the first amendment is with the active speaker, not the passive receiver." Fowler & Brenner, *supra* note 37, at 237–38.

41. "Congress early on decided to abandon market forces in determining grants of exclusivity to the spectrum.... This was the original electromagnetic sin." Ibid. at 212.

Fowler and Brenner do not view the spectrum as necessarily in the public domain; rather they believe that it is possible for frequency rights to be allocable by means of auctions or lotteries with resale occurring without commission involvement. According to this view, spectrum now held in trust for a definite time could be held as private property indefinitely upon its resale. "[T]he marketplace approach could be most expeditiously introduced to broadcasting by granting existing licensees squatter's rights to their frequencies. These rights embody the reasonable expectation of renewal that licensees presently enjoy for satisfactory past performance. The critical next step, from a market viewpoint, would be to deregulate fully the sale of licenses." Ibid. at 244.

42. *Red Lion Broadcasting Co. v. FCC*, 395 U.S. 367 (1969).

43. "Admittedly, there are not unlimited broadcast outlets. But that kind of 'economic scarcity' does not justify content regulation." Text of testimony of FCC Chairman Mark S. Fowler before the Subcommittee on Communications of the Senate Committee on Commerce, Science, and Transportation, March 18, 1987.

44. Dennis R. Patrick and Diane L. Silberstein, "*Red Lion* Still Has Broadcasters Singing the Blues," 3 *Communications Lawyer* 4, 17 (1985): ("there would seem to be no numerical scarcity of broadcast outlets relative to the print media"); *see also, Senate Committee on Commerce, Science, and Transportation: Print and Electronic Media: The Case for First Amendment Parity*; S. Print 98–50, 98th Cong., 1st Sess. 56–69 (1983).

45. "We advocate full first amendment protection for broadcasters not only because broadcasting is indistinguishable from other media for first

amendment purposes, but also because we believe that a marketplace approach to broadcast regulation—parallel to the approach taken nearly two hundred years ago for the print medium—allows broadcasters freedom of speech while ensuring service in the public interest." Mark S. Fowler, "Foreword," 32 *Catholic University Law Review* 523, 525 (1983).

46. *See* A. Smith, *An Inquiry into the Nature and Causes of the Wealth of Nations* (1st ed. Edinburgh, 1776) (Edwin Cannan, ed., 1937) 423.

47. Ibid.

48. "Government oversight of broadcast content...interferes with the functioning of market forces.... [By eliminating such oversight] broadcasters [will be allowed] to satisfy consumer desires based on their reading of what viewers want, from all-news to all-entertainment programming." Fowler & Brenner, supra note 37, at 244–45.

49. *See Steel v. FCC*, No. 84–1176, *supra* (D.C. Cir., ordered remanded October 9, 1986); *Shurburg Broadcasting Co. of Hartford, Inc. v. F.C.C.*, No. 84–1600 (D.C. Cir., ordered remanded Jan. 23, 1987); "Notice of inquiry: In the Matter of Reexamination of the Commission's Comparative Licensing Distress Sales and Tax Certificate Policies Premised on Racial, Ethnic or Gender Considerations," 52 Fed. Reg. 596 (Jan. 7, 1987); *Minority Ownership of Broadcasting Facilities*, 68 F.C.C. 2d 979, 980 n. 8 (1978); *Policy Statement on Comparative Broadcast Hearings*, 1 F.C.C. 2d 393 (1965).

50. Fowler & Brenner, *supra* note 37, at 211.

51. Ibid.

52. *See* DeVany, Eckert, Meyers, O'Hara & Scott, *A Property System for Market Allocation of the Electromagnetic Spectrum: A Legal-Economic-Engineering Study*, 21 Stan. L. Rev. 1499, 1512–22 (1969).

53. Fowler & Brenner, *supra* note 37, at 243.

54. Ibid., at 244.

55. *Deregulation of Radio*, 84 F.C.C. 2d 968 (1981) *recon. granted* in part, 87 F.C.C. 2d 797 (1981) *remanded in part, Office of Communication of the United Church of Christ v. F.C.C.*, 707 F. 2d 1413 (D.C. Cir. 1983); *modified in part*, 57 R.R.2d 93 (1984), *recon. denied*, 96 F.C.C. 2d 930 (1984). *See also, Deregulation of Commercial Television*, 98 F.C.C. 2d 1076 (1984).

56. *Deregulation of Commercial Television*, 98 F.C.C. 2d 1076 (1984).

57. *Deregulation of Radio, supra* note 55, *Deregulation of Commercial Television, supra* note 56.

58. *Deregulation of Commercial Television, supra* note 42.

59. *In re Syracuse Peace Council*, 63 Rad. Reg. 2d (P&F) 541 (1987). The commission first suggested that the fairness doctrine was unconstitutional in *In re Inquiry into Section 73.1910 of the Commission's Rules and Regulations Concerning the General Fairness Doctrine Obligations of Broadcast Licensees*, 102 F.C.C. 2d 143 (1985) (*"1985 Fairness Report"*) but deferred to the judgment of Congress and to the courts on the question of whether the doctrine should continue to be enforced.

60. "The fairness doctrine flows directly from the public trustee notion, and to eliminate the fairness doctrine one must also eliminate the notion that broadcasters should act as public trustees. Moreover, the public trustee notion must be erased before a broadcast journalist can be guaranteed the

same First Amendment rights as a newspaper journalist." Henry Geller, "Broadcasting and the Public Trustee Notion: A Failed Promise," 10 *Harvard Journal of Law and Public Policy* 87 (1987).

61. Portions of this section are derived from Richard Zaragoza and Jonathan Emord, "Electronic Media May Get Same Protection as Print Journalists," *Legal Times*, March 9, 1987, at 15–17.

62. *See Report on Editorializing by Broadcast Licensees, supra* note 21.

63. *See, e.g.*, Ferris and Kirkland, "Fairness—the Broadcaster's Hippocratic Oath," 34 *Catholic University Law Review* 605 (1985); Mitchel, Book Review, 37 *Fed. Comm. L.J.* 377 (1985); Rowan, *Broadcast Fairness: Doctrine Practice Prospects* (1984); Fowler, "Broadcast Unregulation in the 1980's," 119 *Television Q.* 7 (1982); Fowler & Brenner, "A Marketplace Approach to Broadcast Regulation," *supra* note 37; Chamberlain, "FCC and the First Principle of the Fairness Doctrine: A History of Neglect and Distortion," 31 *Fed. Comm. L.J.* 361 (1979); Bazelon, "The First Amendment and the New Media— New Directions in Regulating Telecommunications," 31 *Fed. Comm. L.J.* 201 (1979); Schmidt, *Freedom of the Press vs. Public Access* (1976); Barrow, "Fairness Doctrine: A Double Standard for Electronic and Print Media," 26 *Hasting L.J.* 659 (1975); Bazelon, "FCC Regulation of the Telecommunications Press," 1975 *Duke L.J.* 213 (1975); Geller, *The Fairness Doctrine in Broadcasting* (1973).

64. Upon commission abolition of the doctrine, the chairman of the House Subcommittee on Telecommunications and Finance submitted: "the rancid dish served up today is the same stale stuff that's been ladled out for the last six years....The honeymoon between the Congress and the Patrick Commission is over." *See* Statement by Edward J. Markey, Chairman, U.S. House of Representatives Subcommittee on Telecommunications and Finance, "The Fairness Doctrine and the F.C.C.," released August 4, 1987.

65. *See Communications Daily*, June 4, 1987, at 1; *1985 Fairness Report, supra* note 47, at 247.

66. *In re Syracuse Peace Council*, supra note 59. On the same day that the commission adopted its Memorandum Opinion and Order ending enforcement of the fairness doctrine, it released a "Report of the Commission" to Congress responding to a statutory directive to "consider alternative means of administration and enforcement" of the doctrine. *See Fairness Doctrine Alternatives*, 63 Rad. Reg. 2d (P&F) 488 (1987).

Although enforcement of the general fairness doctrine was ended by the *Syracuse Peace Council* decision, it is unclear whether the decision did encompass other corollaries to it. In a September 22, 1987, letter to John D. Dingell, chairman of the House Committee on Energy and Commerce, FCC Chairman Dennis Patrick explained that "because the enforcement of the political editorial rules, the personal attack rules, the Zapple doctrine, or the application of the fairness doctrine to ballot issues were not before it in *[Syracuse Peace Council]*, the Commission did not make any specific decision on August 4 regarding these issues."

67. In his veto message, President Reagan stated that the fairness doctrine engaged the federal government in "content-based regulation...antagonistic to the freedom of expression guaranteed by the First Amendment....History has shown that the dangers of an overly timid or biased press cannot be

averted through bureaucratic regulation, but only through the freedom and competition that the First Amendment sought to guarantee." Veto Message of the President of June 19, 1987, 23 Weekly Com. Pres. Doc. 715 (June 29, 1987).

68. *See* S. 742. 100th Cong., 1st Sess. (1987); H.R. 1934 (1987).

69. *Broadcasting* magazine's editors asked President Reagan, "If Senator Hollings' fairness doctrine bill is attached to another piece of legislation, would you veto that whole package under those circumstances?" The president responded, "In 1879, the Congress tried to repeal sections of the federal election laws by attaching 'riders' to various appropriations bills, President Rutherford B. Hayes vetoed five successive appropriations bills that summer before Congress finally relented. In his personal diary, Hayes wrote that to abandon principle in the face of this congressional tactic would be to violate a public trust. I do not intend to limit my options, but I will say that I sit at the very desk President Hayes used in the White House—and it may provide some inspiration in the months ahead." See *Broadcasting*, June 29, 1987, at 30. Among proposed amendments considered by Congress to recodify the fairness doctrine is one that would add a new subsection (e) to Section 315 of the Communications Act which would read:

> (e) (1) A broadcast licensee shall afford reasonable opportunity for the discussion of conflicting views on issues of public importance.
>
> (2) The enforcement and application of the requirement imposed by this subsection shall be consistent with the rules and policies of the Commission in effect on January 1, 1987.

70. 47 C.F.R. Sec. 73.1910 (1986). Several corollaries to the fairness doctrine exist. *See* 47 U.S.C. Sec. 312(a)(7); 47 U.S.C. Sec. 315(a); 47 C.F.R. Sec. 76.205; 47 C.F.R. Sec 73.1920; 47 C.F.R. Sec. 1940; *Cullman Broadcasting Co., Inc.*, 25 Rad. Reg. (P&F) 895 (1963).

71. *Report on Editorializing by Broadcast Licensees, supra* note 21, at 1248.

72. Ibid., at 1249.

73. Ibid., at 1258.

74. 47 U.S.C. Sec. 315(a): (the essential purpose of this section is to afford bona fide candidates an "equal opportunity" to "use" a broadcast station, if an opposing candidate is permitted to have such "use." The amendment was primarily designed to exempt from the "equal opportunity" rule bona fide newscasts, news interview programs, on-the-spot coverage of news events, and news documentaries).

75. *See* Act of Sept. 14, 1959, Sec. 1, Pub. L. No. 66–274, 73 Stat. 556 *amending* 47 U.S.C. Sec. 315 (n) (emphasis added).

76. *See, e.g.* 102 F.C.C. 2d at 187, 231.

77. *See Telecommunications Research and Action Center v. FCC*, 801 F.2d 501, 516 (D.C. Cir.), *pet. for reh. en banc denied*, 806 F.2d 111 (D.C. Cir. 1986), *cert. denied*, 55 U.S. L.W 3821 (U.S. 1987), wherein the D.C. Circuit determined that the fairness doctrine was a regulatory policy not a statutory requirement.

78. 105 Cong. Rec. 14,457 (1959).

79. Ibid.

80. *Fairness Doctrine: Hearings on S. 251, S. 252, S. 1696, and H.J. Res.*

247 *Before the Subcomm. on Communications of the Senate Comm. on Commerce*, 88th Cong., 1st Sess. 59 (1963).

81. S. Rep. No. 562, at 13 (1959).

82. H.R. Rep. No. 1069, 86th Cong., 1st Sess. (1959), 86th Cong., 1st Sess. 105 Cong. Rec. 17, 778–832 (1959).

83. *See, e.g.*, 105 Cong. Rec. 17,778–79, 17,781, 17,830–32 (1959).

84. 395 U.S. at 380, *see, e.g.*, 105 Cong. Rec. 17,831–32 (1959).

85. 395 U.S. at 375.

86. Ibid., at 390.

87. *See, e.g., Miami Herald Publishing Co. v. Tornillo*, 418 U.S. 241, 258 (1974) (in which a Florida Statute compelling newspapers to afford a right of reply to political candidates they assail in print was held an unconstitutional abridgment of the First Amendment "because of its intrusion into the function of editors;" no effort was made to distinguish *Red Lion Broadcasting*).

88. 395 U.S. at 388.

89. Ibid., at 393.

90. Ibid., at 388.

91. Ibid., at 380.

92. 47 U.S.C. Subsections 303, 303(r); 395 U.S. at 379.

93. *Fairness Report*, 48 F.C.C. 2d 1 (1974); *recon.denied*, 36 Rad. Reg. 2d (P&F) 1023, *remanded in part*, 567 F.2d 1095 (D.C. Cir. 1977).

94. 468 U.S. 364 (1984).

95. *Id.* at 376–77, n.11 (emphasis added).

96. 102 F.C.C. 2d 143.

97. Ibid., at 147.

98. Ibid.

99. Ibid.

100. Ibid.

101. Ibid.

102. 809 F.2d 863 (D.C. Cir. 1987).

103. 801 F.2d 501 (D.C. Cir. 1987).

104. Robert H. Bork was nominated by President Ronald Reagan to be the 104th Justice to serve on the United States Supreme Court. The Senate voted against his nomination. He has resigned as a Judge on the D.C. Circuit.

105. Then Circuit Judge Antonin Scalia, now an Associate Justice of the United States Supreme Court, joined Judge Bork in the majority opinion of the court.

106. Teletext is a new communications technology that permits over-the-air transmission of text and high-resolution graphics (not accompanied by audio) between the pulses of the regular television vertical blanking interval. Teletext is capable of being received by viewers using a special teletext decoding device on their television sets.

107. Contemplating what the Supreme Court might do if presented again with the issue of spectrum scarcity validity, Bork indicated that the Court might well find it entirely untenable or would "announce a constitutional distinction that is more usable than the present one." 801 F.2d at 509.

108. 801 F.2d at 508.

109. Certiorari in *TRAC v. FCC* was denied, see 55 U.S.L.W. 3821 (U.S. 1987).

110. 809 F.2d 863 (D.C. Cir. 1987).

111. 59 Rad. Reg. 2d (P&F) 179 (1985).

112. 99 F.C.C. 2d 1389, 1401 (1984).

113. Ibid.

114. 59 Rad. Reg. 2d at 181.

115. Ibid., at 185.

116. 809 F.2d 863, 868 (D.C. Cir. 1987).

117. Ibid., at 871.

118. Ibid., at 873.

119. Ibid., at 874.

120. Ibid.

121. Ibid.

122. *Order Requesting Comment*, FCC 87–33, released January 23, 1987.

123. *See Commission Meeting Agenda*, released July 28, 1987; *see News Release*, "FCC Ends Enforcement of Fairness Doctrine" (separate Statement of Chairman Dennis R. Patrick), released August 4, 1987.

124. *In re Syracuse Peace Council*, 63 Rad. Reg. 2d (P&F) at 543. The commission reiterated as a basis for its decision the findings of the 1985 Fairness Report that the doctrine " 'chills' speech . . . , 'operates as a pervasive and significant impediment to the broadcasting of controversial issues of public importance[,] inhibit[s] the expression of unpopular opinion[,] . . . places the government in the intrusive role of scrutinizing program content[,] creates the opportunity for abuse for partisan political purposes[,] and . . . imposes unnecessary costs upon both broadcasters and the Commission.' " Ibid., at 544.

125. *See* Veto Message of the President, 23 Weekly Comp. Pres. Doc. 715 (June 29, 1987).

126. *See* S. 742, 100th Cong., 1st Sess. (1987).

127. Just three days after the commission voted to end enforcement of the fairness doctrine, the Media Access Project filed a Notice of Appeal of the decision in behalf of the Syracuse Peace Council in the U.S. Court of Appeals, New York. *See Syracuse Peace Council v. FCC and USA*, Case No. 87–4098 (2nd Cir., 1987).

128. Suggestions that *currently* allocated spectrum be auctioned raise potentially serious problems of disruption of service to the public, for current licensees would be forced to abandon use of their spectrum if they were unable to afford its market price. This outcome coupled with the apparent inequity of depriving current broadcasters of the value of their good faith reliance upon and investment in allocated spectrum has rendered the option disfavored by many.

3

PUBLIC INTEREST: A WAY OF BROADCAST LIFE

The president of the National Association of Broadcasters, Edward Fritts, points out in this chapter that while public interest may be a congressional mandate, it is actually a way of life for the broadcaster. Although there may be a variety of different activities in the public interest, depending on the station, this "way of broadcast life" has come to mean serving the broadcaster's community. He asserts that despite the present period of increasing federal deregulation, community service and broadcasting will continue to go hand in hand.

One might observe in reading this article that there are some interesting similarities between broadcasting and other forms of local community service. For example, this nation has traditionally placed its basic education within a local milieu. This local emphasis on education is taken for granted. Although broadcasters must answer to the Federal Communications Commission, their successful compliance, like that of the school systems everywhere, is measured by how well they serve the local community.

Whatever the programming, whatever the cause, the successful broadcaster specifically applies the public-interest concept to meet local needs. Of course, Edward Fritts, as president of a national organization, writes in general terms for broadcasters nationwide—a message for all—that public interest means community interest. And one might add, whether the station is located in a large or a small market, that meaning remains exactly the same. Throughout this book, the public-interest obligation is measured in both community activity and in dollars and cents.

About the Author

Edward O. Fritts became nineteenth president of the National Association of Broadcasters (NAB) in October 1982, having previously held a number of board and committee positions including joint chairman of the NAB Board. The son of a small-market radio operator, he was raised in broadcasting. He is former president and owner of Fritts Broadcasting, a group of four AM and four FM stations, including WNLA AM/FM in his hometown of Indianola, Mississippi.

In January 1986 President Reagan appointed Fritts as chairman of the President's Commission on Private Sector Initiatives. He serves on the Board of Directors of the National Commission Against Drunk Driving in Washington, D.C., and sits on the Board of Directors of the Advertising Council, the Museum of Broadcasting, and the Management Board of the Media-Advertising Partnership for a Drug-Free America, all in New York City. He was chairman of the Media Advisory Committee to the U.S. Bicentennial Commission and a member of the Voice of America Broadcast Advisory Committee.

Edward Fritts is an advisory trustee for the Southern Baptist Abe Lincoln Awards Program, Fort Worth, Texas, and as an "Ole Miss" alumnus, serves on the board of the University of Mississippi Foundation. He was recently awarded the Highest Effort Award from the National Sigma Alpha Epsilon Fraternity.

Broadcasters and the Public Interest

EDWARD O. FRITTS

Serving the public interest is more than a mandate handed down by Congress. It is a self-imposed credo by which successful broadcasters operate their stations. It is the touchstone of American broadcasting.

Serving the public interest takes many forms at radio and television stations across the country. It is the statewide telethon-radiothon sponsored by West Virginia stations in 1985 to raise $900,000 for victims of a flood that ravaged the state. It is the live, prime-time debates, sponsored during the 1986 elections by WJLA-TV in Washington, D.C., between Maryland senatorial candidates who fielded questions from a panel of three area political reporters. It is national syndicated radio talk/call-in shows, such as Mutual's "Larry King Show," entertaining audiences throughout the night with his personal style of informative newsmaker interviews. It is the high school football and basketball radio play-by-play coverage provided by WHOP since 1940 in Hopkinsville, Kentucky.

Programming in the "public interest, convenience or necessity," as stated in the Communications Act, is a way of broadcast life. Whether that means responsiveness to the needs and interests of the local community, contributing to discussion of important issues, presentation of high-quality programming, or encouragement of free speech, it carries with it a special obligation to provide information and service to the local audience.

Broadcasters recognize that the responsibility to serve the public interest is inherent in holding their license, and it is also a vital ingredient for success. In a one-station market, there is no question of serving the community, because the station is the voice of the community. In larger markets, competition is so intense that the broadcasters must reflect the interests of the community or risk being turned out in favor of their competitors.

Broadcasting is the public's major source of information about what is happening in today's world. Such programming as public affairs shows; news, weather, and sports reports; special programming for children and minorities; editorials; documentaries; political coverage; agricultural reports; and religious programming contribute to the overall welfare of a broadcaster's audience. Broadcasters become fused with their local communities not only through coverage of local news and events, but also through on-air access accorded to the public and through personal involvement of station personnel in community activities.

I've lived my entire life in broadcasting—as the son of a respected radio station broadcaster who started out in the pioneering days of the medium, as the owner/operator of a group of small-market radio stations in the South, and now, as president of the association that represents the television and radio industry. I've known thousands of broadcasters along the way. What I have learned is that there is a dedication to serving the public, to serving the local community, that is not unique to any one individual or particular group of broadcasters. It is a common thread that binds them together and makes our American system of broadcasting the best in the world.

My personal legacy, handed down to me by my father, ingrained in me the notion that to be successful, a station has to be a reflection of the community it serves. Operations should be geared to allow a maximum opportunity for local expression. When a station is tuned into the community, listeners and viewers identify with that station and support it.

Successful stations cover the local scene: agriculture reports, basketball highlights, local politics, livestock shows, spelling bees, arts festivals. Local stations are the principal local news outlets in the communities, with all the attendant bells and whistles—wire services, state news network, national network, mobile news van—to assure the most professional and up-to-date news service possible.

In times of crisis, audiences tune to their local stations for emergency information. When a hurricane or tornado hits, during fires and floods, communities rely on their local radio and TV stations—in many instances, their only source of news and information. Local stations will often suspend their regular programming to serve as an information network for updates on the disaster, how to get supplies, who should report to work, whether the water is drinkable, emergency shelter availability—in general, a community coping mechanism.

It is crucial to maintain good relationships with all segments of the community—minorities, the elderly, handicapped—all of whom have opportunities for expression on their local stations. Public access is available in a variety of forms, including public affairs shows, community forums, call-in programs, public service announcements aired free of charge. Such access assures that the views of all segments of the community are represented.

The political scene is also covered extensively at the local stations to help citizens make informed choices when they enter the voting booth. Local stations provide an outlet for candidate interviews and political forums on state and local issues; they may even sponsor political debates. Broadcasters recognize the important role that they play in making the American political process work.

Community involvement is more than on-air reports. Station personnel are encouraged to participate in a wide variety of community activities. They serve on the Chamber of Commerce, visit hospitals, coach the Little League, organize the leukemia drive, join the neighborhood council. At one time, our news director was even the vice mayor of the city. Identification with the local community is essential for a broadcaster, not only because it serves the public, but also because it is good business. A station that remains sensitive to the true concerns and interests of its community—which it can only do through active participation—will merit the confidence and support of its audience.

What I have discovered throughout my career, as I met with fellow broadcasters at industry conventions and participated in committees of my state broadcast association and NAB, is that public service is the normal course of business for the vast majority of radio and television stations around the country. As broadcasters, we take very seriously our responsibilities to our communities.

In the past five years, the Federal Communications Commission has acted to deregulate parts of the broadcast industry, freeing it from burdensome and onerous paperwork and allowing it, as well as other competing technologies, to grow in a more unfettered environment. The question has been posed, will stations in the absence of government-imposed regulation, remain sensitive to the needs and interests of the public? The answer, quite simply, is yes.

The public interest standard remains. A station is judged at license renewal time on fulfillment of its public-interest responsibilities and its community programming. Our industry has strongly supported the public-interest standard and the obligations it implies.

Further, we are in the midst of a communications revolution. Driven by technology, electronic delivery systems such as cable and satellite have created a nearly unlimited number of signals with which the local broadcast station must compete. What differentiates us from competitive technologies is our ability to mirror the lives of our community, to reflect their needs and interests in our programming and community activities.

The competition from within is also intense. With nearly 10,000 commercial stations in operation—almost six times the number of daily newspapers—the real challenge is to offer something unique to our audiences.

As the sounding board of the community, local radio and television stations position themselves as involved leaders. The work they do is vitally important to their communities and to the nation.

In my travels around the country representing NAB, I have had an opportunity to appear on a number of public affairs programs. The creativity, ingenuity, and zeal that the bright minds in our business apply to their profession is impressive.

For the past several years, as an extension of industry activities, NAB has regularly increased its role in providing public service campaigns for stations. The association has targeted a few special issues and developed campaigns at the national level that can be adapted by stations in local communities. The extraordinarily positive response by broadcasters proves our industry's continuing commitment to the public interest.

Separate campaigns have focused on voter awareness during the 1984 election, American productivity, drunk driving, and drug and alcohol abuse. Broadcasters' outstanding drunk driving campaigns of the past few years have earned praise from every sector. While these voluntary initiatives are part of our responsibility to serve the public, the rewards reach beyond commendations. Social attitudes toward those who drive drunk or impaired are changing, for instance, and broadcasters have made a significant contribution to the educational process, which is effecting that change.

NAB has teamed up with government agencies, professional athletes, coaches, parents, schools, and kids to warn of the dangers of drugs. Stations all across the U.S. have joined us to bring to every home in America a clear antidrug message. By airing PSA's and public affairs shows and creating community awareness campaigns, broadcasters are attempting to educate the public on the perils of drug abuse, thereby enhancing the quality of life in their communities. These are just a few examples of the thousands of ways stations serve their audiences.

The concept of serving the public interest permeates daily broadcast life. It is a concept we are proud to live by for the good of American broadcasting and the nation as a whole. Broadcasters don't pretend to be the saviors of the world, but we attempt to contribute to the betterment of society. Harry Truman liked to recall an epitaph in the cemetery at Tombstone, Arizona, which read: "Here lies Jack Williams. He done his damedest." When it's all said and done, we would like to believe that we have done our "damnedest" for our community, our nation, and for future generations.

4

TELEVISION
RATINGS

Few companies have had the profound effect on the American way of life as the A. C. Nielsen Company. Since the average home has the television set turned on for more than seven hours daily, and since broadcasters compete for as much of the audience as they can attract, Nielsen ratings play a significant role in determining for the broadcasters the reach of their programming.

Those who object to broadcasters using such a service forget that the broadcasting industry in this country operates in a competitive marketplace just like other commercial businesses, where the public ultimately determines the acceptability of the product. Certainly broadcasting is a different, more persuasive—and for many, more influential—than most other services, but federal legislation long ago created our broadcast service as a competitive, commercial enterprise. This nation's broadcasting is, with the singular exception of a much smaller public broadcast system, commercial. Within that framework the commercial broadcaster has a public-interest obligation. But first a business must survive and profit amid competitors. Ratings measure the success of that survival.

As long as the free marketplace of ideas is linked to the commercial marketplace where competition and profit are the dominant forces, television ratings will be necessary. Public-interest obligations, therefore, must be harnessed to the machine of commerce if the broadcaster is to thrive. That is the reality of American broadcasting.

About the Author

Arthur C. Nielsen is the former chairman of the Board and chief executive officer of the A. C. Nielsen Company, a marketing research organization best known for its television broadcasting research, but also serving the food, drug, pharmaceutical, tobacco, confectionary, publishing, oil and gas, and other high-tech industries.

Nielsen is a graduate in business administration of the University of Wisconsin, where he won high honors for his scholastic and extra-curricular activities. In 1977 he was selected for *Financial World's* award as one of the top chief executive officers of the year in the business service world. In 1980 he was named outstanding chief executive officer in the business service field by *The Wall Street Transcript*. Among the many awards he has received are: Distinguished Alumnus of the University of Wisconsin, 1982; the Distinguished Service Award from the Wisconsin Alumni Association, 1983; and Laureate in the Lincoln Academy of Illinois, 1984.

He has served as an advisor to three presidents as well as a marketing consultant to the U.S. government. He served in the U.S. Army during World War II, rising to the rank of major in the Corps of Engineers. During this time he received the Legion of Merit.

Nielsen is chairman of the Board of the Museum of Broadcast Communications in Chicago, and serves on the board of directors of other corporations including Motorola, Walgreen Company, and Dun & Bradstreet.

Television Ratings and the Public Interest

ARTHUR C. NIELSEN, JR.

Television may be the greatest invention of the past 500 years. Everyone wants a TV set. Even the poorest families all over the world buy them. Viewing in the United States exceeds seven hours per household per day. Its impact on all our lives can hardly be overestimated.

It has been said that the television industry lives or dies based on Nielsen ratings. Is this true? If so, are the ratings "good" or "bad," and how did the A.C. Nielsen Company ever get into such a powerful position, anyway? Perhaps the following remarks will throw some light on these questions.

Our company began measuring radio listening following the Second World War in an effort to help manufacturers increase the efficiency of their advertising. The "rating" was merely an estimate of the number of households listening to an individual program. Television ratings came later, of course, but our objective remained the same.

The need for such a system, and the estimates it could provide, developed as an outgrowth of the industrial revolution and the accompanying increase in production. Vast quantities of goods could be produced in factories at very low cost, and standards of living rose all over the industrialized world. As the number of different products offered consumers increased, it became more difficult for manufacturers to sell any particular product because buyers were presented with so many choices. Advertising developed to facilitate the movement of all these products from the factory to the home. In short, the benefits of mass production could not exist without the aid of mass advertising. For this reason, advertising has become an important part of the means by which goods are distributed. In fact, over half of the price we must pay for the things we buy today is made up of distribution costs which include advertising, transportation, warehousing and retailing.

To the extent that the process of distribution can be made more efficient, products can be sold at a lower cost thereby providing a higher standard of living for all. For this reason, it became important for the advertiser to direct his sales message to those people who are most likely to buy his product.

Now, unfortunately, when a commercial is aired on radio or television, it goes out over the airwaves, and without ratings no one would know how many people received the message or if they were the best prospects for the product being advertised. To be successful an advertiser must find out which programs appeal to potential customers and then select the program that reaches that audience at the lowest cost. This is the purpose and function performed by the Nielsen ratings.

In short, with the help of the Nielsen ratings, advertisers can sell their goods and services at the lowest possible price, keep their factories running smoothly, and provide employment for their workers and a fair return to their shareholders for the capital required in the business. Ratings are an essential part of this overall system. For this reason I believe that they operate in the public interest because they do contribute to a higher standard of living. Few who know how modern business operates would, I believe, dispute this claim.

There is, however, a second function performed by the ratings, which is more controversial. I refer to the fact that the broadcaster uses ratings to determine the type of programs to be carried by the networks and stations. The Nielsen Company did not have this function in mind when it first offered its service. It seems to me that this particular use arose because advertising revenues are the means used in this country to pay for operating television stations and networks.

Since what the broadcaster has to sell is an audience to advertisers, it follows that in order to attract viewers, the broadcaster must cater to the public tastes and preferences. Ratings reveal these preferences. Some decry this system, claiming it leads to programming that appeals to the lowest common denominator—that programs of educational and cultural merit are given short shrift.

This was obviously a legitimate concern, and so in order to safeguard the public interest, the government in granting a license to broadcast provided certain guidelines that have led to a diversity of programming. The viewer will find, in fact, many programs which are known to have limited appeal including religion, news, and public service.

Since a license to broadcast has considerable commercial value, the owners of stations are most anxious to retain this privilege and so strive to operate in the public interest by offering a great diversity of program choices. For example, in my home town of Chicago, in one typical week this past year there were 4,650 different programs from which one could choose.

Furthermore, those who feel that broadcasters carry programs with too much violence, sex, or not enough educational fare for children have been successful in organizing themselves to make their beliefs effectively known and respected by broadcasters. Some products such as hard liquor and cigarettes, for example, are not advertised on television. Various trade associations concerned with advertising have also made their wishes known by establishing various codes of conduct, which carry considerable weight with broadcasters. In this way the government, as well as various public and private groups, influences what we see on television. Ratings are but one of a number of such influences.

I am familiar with television in other countries where government agencies do exercise more control over programming and advertising than is the case here in the United States. My observation has been that these systems tend to become bureaucratic and that the public receives whatever the government believes is good for them. In most cases, advertising is restricted, and the cost of programming is provided out of revenues collected from taxes on set owners. The result has been that the programs offered seem to have less general appeal. I conclude this from the fact that the number of hours viewed by the typical family is considerably less than here in the United States.

Some advocate government intervention in broadcasting in the belief that the public will be exposed to fine, more elevating types of programming. Unfortunately, one man's meat is too often another man's poison, and even the experts seem unable to agree as to what is best for all of us.

I believe that the system of broadcasting that has evolved here in the United States is the best for us. It is based upon the democratic principle of free choice that is so fundamental to our way of life. With the help of ratings, broadcasters know what we find most appealing and desire to view. Broadcasters have every incentive to please the public. Each of us votes every day by the simple process of turning our dials. What could be more democratic?

5

FIRST SERVE THE PUBLIC

The network perspective, as seen through the eyes of the president of the CBS/Broadcast Group, embraces the long view, the overview, of the role of public interest in broadcasting. At first it would appear that everything can be translated into dollars and cents, programming "contests," advertising, and concerns over the encroachment of federal regulation into broadcast competition. However, beneath the surface and the glitter of network operations has been the evolution of this dynamic form of communication that ultimately ends with the aired program and the competition it faces.

As impressive as the financial statistics that describe the business of broadcasting are, Gene Jankowski points out that they should not obscure the public-interest obligation. The "first premise," and the best business practice for which there is no substitute, is to serve the public interest.

One might conclude from his description that there is little difference between marketing of goods and telecasting popular programs, but that conclusion would be wrong. In the marketplace where ideas, tastes, values, and influence compete, television must still account for the public interest. The average viewer has walked on the moon, been part of a war, felt the sadness of death, and experienced the despair of the hungry and homeless, thanks to television. Television has at times also trivialized personal and social relationships, catered to morbid curiosity, and offered programs of low artistic quality. First Amendment rights have been exercised superbly, sometimes irresponsibly.

About the Author

Gene F. Jankowski has been president of the CBS/Broadcast Group since 1977. He is responsible for all the broadcast activities of CBS Inc.

He joined CBS in 1961 as an account executive with CBS Radio Network Sales, becoming eastern sales manager in 1966. In 1969 he joined the CBS Television Network Sales Department as an account executive, and in 1970 was appointed general sales manager of WCBS-TV, New York. The following year he became director of sales at the station. In 1973 he became vice president of sales for CBS Television Stations Division, and 1974 was appointed the division's vice president for finance and planning. He was named vice president and controller of CBS Inc. in 1976 and retained that position until his appointment as vice president for administration in 1977. Later that same year, he was named executive vice president of the CBS/Broadcast Group.

Jankowski has received the Distinguished Communications Medal, the highest honor bestowed by the Southern Baptist Radio and Television Commission; an honorary Doctorate of Humanities from Michigan State University; and the Humanitarian Award of the National Conference of Christians and Jews.

He is a trustee of the American Film Institute; a trustee of the Catholic University of America; a director of Georgetown University; a member of the Board of Governors of the American Red Cross; a member of the National Board of Directors of Boys Hope; and vice chairman of the Business Committee of the Metropolitan Museum of Art.

The Broadcast Industry's First Premise: Serve the Public

GENE F. JANKOWSKI

An inauguration, a summit, a budget. Terrorism: in the air, at sea, at airports. Natural disasters: hurricanes, volcanoes, earthquakes. Air disasters: the worst year ever. Human triumphs in science, medicine, and technology. Human spirit: in Live Aid and Farm Aid. Pop culture: Rambo, Springsteen, Madonna. Sports culture: Pete Rose, Villanova, the Bears.

In the year 1985 some things were not always what they seemed. Many of us discovered that "The Boss" wasn't necessarily in an office, and "The Refrigerator" wasn't always in the kitchen.

It was a year that the American public depended on broadcasters more than ever for news and information, and broadcasters provided them with more coverage than ever before. For entertainment, audience level increased as people spent more time with television and radio.

There was also plenty of activity behind the scenes in our business, and that is what I'd like to talk about today. It also starts with some images:

Helms and Westmoreland; beer and wine advertising; Cap Cities and ABC; the arbitrageurs and analysts; KKR and Storer; Turner and CBS?; Murdoch and Fox and Metromedia; Gannett and Evening News Association; Turner and NBC?; Taft and Gulf; Tribune and KTLA; Turner and *Time*?; Viacom and MTV; Lorimar and Telepictures,

From a speech before the International Radio & Television Society Newsmaker Luncheon, at the Waldorf-Astoria Hotel, New York, January 15, 1986.

Turner and Viacom?; 1988 Olympics; Buying CBS News?; Turner and MGM?; GE and RCA.

Put the year's media transactions all together and they spell MONEY—to the tune of an estimated $30 billion! It all sounds like the ultimate "Wheel of Fortune."

Indeed 1985 was an incredible year. This halfway point in the decade was the time Wall Street discovered our industry ... and when they did the Gold Rush was on. Mergers and acquisitions, leveraged buy-outs, financing and refinancing, stock offerings, stock buy-backs ... you name it. It was a year when Wall Street analysts made more appearances on "Entertainment Tonight" than network presidents. And we spent as much time following the Dow Jones wire, *Barrons* and *Business Week* as we did *Broadcasting* and *Variety*.

It's easy to see how our industry today is quite different from the one that many of us grew up in; it's different today than it was twelve months ago. What is also different is the increasing amount of time and activity spent by all sorts of media covering our business.

All this attention is flattering and, at times, frustrating and distracting. While it's nice to know that the experts in the investment world agree that the future health of our industry is bright, and while it's interesting to watch and read about the goings-on of our business, we also have to put up with the gossip and speculation, too. We live in a fishbowl that seems to grow larger each year. In fact, I can think of only one other organization that receives such wide coverage on everything from office policy to office politics ... and that's the government.

What we must not forget in all of this is *perspective*—a frame of reference about the business, where it came from and where it may be going. I'd like to share that with you today in a thumbnail outline of the business from its beginnings until now. It divides itself into three distinct areas, one I will call Television One, Two, and Three.

Television One: Coming of Age

The first period, Television One, covers the years 1950 through 1975. It was a quarter century of uninterrupted growth. Like any new medium, television began by using the content of its predecessors— radio, newspapers, books, theater, and the movies. This created the audience and revenue base needed to move into an extended cycle of self-development. The medium set out to invent itself.

CBS and NBC were the major players in this process. They were in full confrontation in most areas, but they also had established franchises in others. ABC was an enterprising third—a spirited but not-quite-equal competitor struggling with limited resources.

Toward the end of this period, in the early 1970s, a series of severe regulatory restrictions was imposed on the networks (Prime Time Access Rule, Financial Interest and Syndication, Cross Ownership, and others). However, it was to be some time before these regulations had substantial effect.

In brief, through this quarter of a century the networks occupied a stable and clearly defined space that contained its own growth potential. It was a space in which movement was easy to track; in which competitive gains and losses were traded directly by the participants and in which the driving forces remained constant. The business grew larger, but its dynamics did not change.

Television Two: The Territorial Imperative

This phase was triggered by the emergence of ABC as a full-scale competitor. A new level of three-network competition broke out. Every day part was severely contested. Station, talent, and rights wars began. Promotion, advertising, and marketing efforts were intensified. There were second and even third seasons. Sweeps became network programming contests. All of this produced radical cost and price escalation. These increases were absorbed by an inflationary economy, a history of what had probably been underpricing and lack of alternatives. By 1980, only half a decade after Television Two appeared, a new configuration began to take shape. Television Three arrived.

Television Three: Action and Reaction

Television Three introduced structural change. It is generally identified with the appearance and growth of the "new technologies," and they were the distinguishing factor, but they did not act in the manner immediately expected. They did not displace the networks or even compete with them directly, but they did affect the networks. Arriving against the backdrop of the earlier restrictive regulation, they became another restraint on growth opportunities while simultaneously introducing new forms of competition.

The pattern was complex, unfolding in several stages. The networks had been barred from cable ownership, program ownership, syndication and expansion in prime time a decade earlier. These were negatives that put limits on eventual growth opportunities, although their impact was delayed. However, exclusion from cable was one thing; the growth of cable was another. This had a positive effect for competitive forces. It strengthened the market position of independents by eliminating the technological handicaps of UHF's and helped give syndication an entirely new economic dimension.

At the end of this chain reaction, the networks found themselves barred from a significant revenue stream flowing from the very products whose value they had established. Nonetheless, they were compelled to continue investing in that product, at ever-increasing costs.

It was an ironic position. The desire for better reception of network programming continued to be an essential ingredient in the growth of cable. That same network programming in a rerun afterlife was also the backbone of the syndication marketplace, which was being expanded through the growth of cable. So the networks found themselves paying a double penalty for their own investment in creativity. They funded the development process that fueled a growing marketplace from which they were excluded.

Looking at all of this, some traditional business school analysts defined television as a "mature" business. That may be true on a rather narrow perspective. However, the same thing could have been said about radio some time ago. Yet 1985 was radio's best year ever.

As far as television is concerned, it may be more accurate to say that television as we know it seems to be a "mature" business simply because it is already so abundant, so available, so technologically sophisticated, so energetic and so accepted that it is hard to imagine it becoming even more so. Which is also what a lot of people were saying twenty years ago. And today, if this is maturity, it seems to be the envy of a very significant portion of the business world.

That brings me to the most startling aspect of Television Three. A series of regulatory decisions ultimately had a collective impact of enormous consequence. Ownership rules changed, and stations were put into the open marketplace.

Broadcasting people woke up to discover that they were sitting on the top of the San Andreas Fault (or that gold, diamonds, and oil had all been found on their property at once—whichever you prefer). None of the other changes have the same kind of unsettling effects as this one—at least potentially—and the process is far from complete.

This is a change in kind, not just in degree. Television Three is a shift from a two-dimensional to a three-dimensional world. This new marketability of the broadcast license is just one element in the shift. Certain of the Federal Communications Commission's regulations from the last decade combined with today's deregulation have also created unexpected interactions between the traditional broadcast universe and the "new technologies." Finally, the "new technologies" themselves have had direct and indirect competitive impacts in various degrees of predictability—and unpredictability.

At the same time, some basic elements—programming, technologies and regulatory actions for instance—are traveling simultane-ously. And out beyond all this is the circle of investors, arbitrageurs, merger-makers and takeover specialists, a mega-force entirely new to the industry.

A good symbol for this new order might be the "double helix," the famous model of the DNA molecule. It looks like a spiral staircase without the steps. We still have discrete industry segments—stations, networks, production companies, agencies, clients, and so on at the core, but the functional elements of our business no longer relate themselves to these segments in the traditional manner.

Instead, those elements wrap themselves around the core, inter-facing with it in different ways at different places. For example, VCR's affect commercial broadcasters one way, cable operators another, and production companies yet another. So various regulatory and legis-lative developments. And all of them play into the financial world differently. In these circumstances, competitive postures are not rigid or consistent. Instead, combination and recombination become the style. And, indeed, that is what we are beginning to see all around us.

That's the part that has changed. As we look at all this, it is im-portant to consider as well those things that have not changed . . . and that are, in a sense, not changeable. One of these, for example, is the output process that feeds the entire industry. It is a process with four components—development, production, distribution, and funding. This is the chain reaction that drives the medium in all its aspects, new or old. There has to be a reliable way to find new product. There has to be a reliable way to produce it. There has to be a reliable way to get it to our audiences. There has to be a reliable way to pay for it.

These functions flow into each other. They must have a stable and systematic relationship to each other. And, most important, to have television as we know it, they must have adequate scale. This is a point that cannot be made too often. We are talking about an *annual* supply of television programs for prime time alone that equals ten years of Hollywood film output or twenty-five years of Broadway theatrical performances.

For the industry, in Television One, Two, and Three, the keeper of this process has been the network–affiliate partnership. Without its output—without nearly 15,000 hours of network programming per year distributed continuously across a national base—it is hard to see how the other parts of the structure could have developed as they have. For example, it is difficult to imagine Community Antenna Television developing to a point where a cable industry could emerge. Or how independent stations would have achieved the status they have today. Or what would have driven the market for VCR's, if not for the taping and time shifting of network programs.

This partnership has stood the test of time for only one reason: it serves the public. It satisfies their needs and responds to their interests. All broadcasting succeeds for that reason and that reason alone. And that is the final immutable fact.

That may seem obvious, but it bears repeating. That principle hasn't changed, but the world around it has. For example, the Federal Communications Commission is now making decisions with incalculable consequences on the basis of its interpretation of "shareholder democracy." Who amongst us would have dared to predict that even five years ago?

I am not trying to evaluate any of these decisions. But I am saying that this is very strange new ground for the FCC to occupy. It is a very long way from frequencies and transmitters or licenses or even the radio speaker or the television screen. But I would also suggest that no one here could have anticipated that financial investments would become an issue of decisive importance to the commission. Investment concerns are not, in my view, an adequate substitute for the public interest. Investors are best served when we best serve the public. This is the fundamental concept of the broadcasting business, its first premise.

Broadcasters share a relationship and trust with the American public. And we will continue to succeed or fail by how well we can serve and satisfy their needs. We must not lose sight of that in the new world of Television Three.

As far as the future is concerned, I am very optimistic. The interest in our business will continue from Main Street to Wall Street from Madison Avenue to Sunset Boulevard and all points in between. As the marketplace continues to become even more competitive, the level of product will rise, and so will audience response.

You are entitled to ask whether that is unjustified optimism—a necessary but unfelt response to corporate tradition. Let me ask you to perform a small exercise. Imagine that the thumbnail history I have described had a different configuration. Assume that no cable industry ever developed . . . that independent stations did not increase and instead remained on the fringes of the business . . . that no satellites had ever gone up . . . that there was no such thing as a VCR. Would you be more or less optimistic about the future of broadcasting? I believe the answer is less optimistic. And yet I am only suggesting an industry in which none of the so-called competitors to the networks exist. I think you would find that a sadly depleted and unexciting world. And so would I.

So would you call network television a static business today?

Hardly! One must remember that when Mr. Paley started CBS, people were still listening to crystal radio sets. Now we have color television pictures sent back from spaceships circling the globe.

And now, this medium is entering yet another revolutionary phase. Mobile uplinks can provide the means to weave a daily tapestry of local, regional, national, and international news of incredible depth and complexity, and satellite footprints cover continents. In this environment the opportunities to grow cannot be limited if we have skill, knowledge, and imagination.

The point is that each of these waves of innovation, growth and competition enriched all of us ... because they enriched the screen ... and therefore the public. Not only is that process still with us, it is more vigorous than ever. That's why I look forward eagerly to Television Four ... and Five ... and Six.

The message should be quite clear to this and the next generation in our industry: As good as our business is today, the best is yet to come.

6

THE EVOLVING CONCEPT

The confusion over what the term "public interest" means precisely can be put into proper perspective if broadcasting is recognized as a commercial system that operates on its own without content control by the government. According to NBC Vice President Thomas Sawyer, this system leads to "creative tension" between the commercial and public interest objectives that the broadcaster must serve concurrently.

He discusses how the public-interest concept can be interpreted as "uplifting," quality programming, or serving the greatest number of viewers. The legal interpretation as evolved through the legal and legislative action is only part of the concept, and if considered alone, a sterile and confusing guidepost. He attacks those who criticize ratings for appealing to the "faceless mass" as being cynical and inaccurate chiefly because they assume that the audience is made up of passive receivers only. Following more discussion of the loose interpretations of public interest bandied about by politicians, Sawyer offers some specific suggestions for implementing the concept of public interest, urging broadcasters to lobby personally for "policies that would enhance their ability to serve."

The following article offers a number of suggestions worthy of study. Perhaps some broadcasters should at times set aside their individual concerns and make a more united effort to discover what can be done to turn this vague virtue of public interest into an even more effective concept.

About the Author

Thomas C. Sawyer is currently Vice President, Washington operations, for the National Broadcasting Company. Before coming to NBC in 1983, he served as executive vice president of the Ohio Association of Broadcasters. Prior to that time, Sawyer was minority counsel (professional staffer) for the U.S. House of Representatives Subcommittee on Communications.

Holding graduate degrees in journalism and communication from the Ohio State University, Sawyer has co-authored *Communication Now* (Merrill), *The Rhetorical Dialogue* (W. C. Brown), as well as other articles and reviews. He has taught at the University of Wisconsin, George Washington University, and the Ohio State University.

The Evolving Public Interest

THOMAS C. SAWYER

Ironically, while the "public interest" continues to be the cornerstone of our unique system of broadcasting in this country, its definition has always proven elusive. Critics, courts, congressional representatives, consumers, minority groups, lawyers, academicians, and broadcasters have all grappled with the practical meaning of this concept; yet, few have ever reached a total consensus on its nature or implications.

Like many virtuous and noble-sounding general terms, "the public interest" can be the reservoir of many different values, interpretations, and objectives, depending upon one's prejudices, goals, and predispositions. Indeed, much of the lore of the social and behavioral scientists would tell us that our perception of such a term is highly selective, such as, we'll see what we want to see.., hear what we wish to ... in interpreting such general obligations as "operating in the public interest." In practical terms, the concept has developed into a mosaic composed of opinions, values, and interpretations as diverse as the U.S. broadcasting industry and audiences it serves.

While this concept has spawned controversy through the years, it has also anchored a system of radio and television whose stability, success, and qualities are too often taken for granted. So it should be emphasized at the outset that for all its imperfections, hyperbole, and cycles, our broadcasting system remains the best in the world. Though regulated, its content is not controlled by government and

The views and opinions expressed in this essay are strictly personal.

never has been government's or any one party's mouthpiece. Indeed, many newspeople draw regular wrath from both sides of the political aisle for selected stories.

Also, commercial broadcasting in the United States operates on its own financially. It receives zero subsidies from the taxpayer and imposes no direct charges on its viewers and listeners. It offers astounding choice to the consumer as the number of media channels and outlets grows geometrically. Its capability to inform, entertain, link, and reflect cultures is well documented. No, this essay is not intended as a promotion piece for our current system, but seeks to emphasize that however ambiguous and controversial our conceptual guide—"the public interest"—its end product has enviable strengths.

"Creative tension" is no doubt an overworked phrase, but it seems most applicable in beginning our practical look at the public interest. Without belaboring its legal history, our approach to broadcasting in this country has created a tension between two objectives the broadcaster must serve concurrently—operating as a business and serving the public interest. Programming must attract enough audience to sell enough advertising—broadcasters' sole source of income—to be economically viable. Yet, at the same time, the broadcaster must also meet broader needs of audience and locale, operating in the public interest. Serving both objectives can be difficult, yet for most broadcasters and audiences the effort has proven productive.

After working for the congressional committee that dealt with communications policies, then representing stations and a network as their advocate, as well as teaching numerous students of broadcasting, this author would contend that six major sets of influences have helped build the "mosaic" of the public interest. For purposes of stimulating discussion in this essay, these influences can be termed the legalists, altruists, opportunists, practitioners, consumers, and government policy-makers (with some in these groups on occasion indistinguishable from others).

The legalists would have us believe that the public interest is totally driven by considerations of law. Certainly the concept has its foundations in the statutes of our early Communications Acts. Through the years, amendments, court decisions, regulator interpretations, and FCC policy-making have indeed provided the regulatory framework for our industry. Myriad cases and decades of tedious legislative disputes over criteria of station license renewal, levels and indices of performance, and other matters have certainly contributed, however inconsistently and unclearly, to the legal context of the public interest. Yet, if one were to draw narrowly the meaning of our keystone from only the legalists, broadcasting would have to depend on rather sterile and often confusing guideposts.

Usually a more interesting set of influences in defining the public interest comes from the altruists—those who equate the concept almost exclusively with various "higher goods." Many of this school argue that broadcasters prime foci should be "uplifting" educational programming, intellectual stimulation, and attention to underserved needs in society. They have difficulty in squaring a broadcaster's public interest obligations with the business side of the operation. Indeed, some would see little, if any, "legitimate" role for entertainment programming. One congressman of this philosophy argued dramatically in a hearing on broadcast license renewal that only educational broadcasting could serve the public interest, a mission that the profit motive, he stressed, totally "contaminated." Escaping one's self-interest is the key to serving the public well, this school of thought would contend. Several critics in this mode equate the public interest with providing the highest *quality* of programs. Others contend that the public interest is best fulfilled by programming for the needs of minority and other selected interests within the audience. Still others equate the public interest with serving the *greatest number* of citizens well with, for example, news and public affairs programming. Another criterion for success is measured by how much programming is responsive and devoted to local needs. Such advocates frequently draw the response that the media must serve a diversity of needs and interests, that their role and economic reality demand and wider appeal. Still, the "altruists" have provided pressures and direction that have helped stimulate standards of operation that are aimed beyond one's own interest.

Perhaps the most potent force of all on the public interest issue are the media consumers themselves. Many analyses of the forces in broadcasting acknowledge the importance of the audience, often through a scornful swipe at the "ratings" or the need to appeal to the "faceless mass." In fact, one political scientist notes, "mass appeal has its price, namely programming pitched to an anonymous audience whose common characteristics can be assumed and catered to, but whose special interests can neither be known or served."[1] Such assessments are cynically inaccurate and are a disservice to those broadcasting is supposed to serve.

Audience members are not passive gnomes without intelligence or initiative. Research has consistently shown that most are very active consumers. They select, they react, they complain, they reject, and they emphatically express themselves to stations, to their elected representatives, and to networks. And their behavior has massive effects on what's aired and what "the public interest" evolves to be. At NBC, for example, there is a department devoted solely to summarizing and analyzing the reactions of viewers who call and write about shows. The results are summarized weekly for the CEO, senior management, and programming executives. More systematic research is done on specific shows, performers, even on societal trends, worries, and opinions. In addition, an entire Standards Department is constantly assessing what program content and advertising are appropriate for audiences' tastes and values. Individual stations at the local level experience and seek such audience feedback in many more personal ways as their staffs interact with their communities on a daily basis.

Those who attempt to program in the public interest daily would testify to the immense impact of audiences on their thinking. In fact, there is a fascinating body of research that deals with communicators' perceptions of their (1) audience's needs, and (2) the resulting messages. Much of the popular literature on consumers' impact on the public interest deals with "the ratings," usually in a negative light.

Like any measure of complex human behavior, ratings are basically imprecise assessments, but they furnish the best indices we have available as to audience preferences. Ratings are nothing more, and nothing less. Though many researchers and critics may argue over methodologies and accuracies, the ratings have given us good, gross measures of rank-order preferences, trends in viewing, and basic demographic composition of audiences. Though they have enormous impact—probably too much—the fact remains that those who develop shows and those who pay for access to audiences must have some independent measure of "who's out there" for each show. Audience likes and dislikes, now changing more rapidly than ever, have made the popularity of individual shows and networks highly cyclical through the years. Though such feedback may seem at times whimsical, it is essential to any communication process. The ratings—our best available mirror of such audience behavior—have been influential barometers for the industry but hardly the instruments of evil some critic will allege. There's no doubt that the "what works" value illustrated by this ongoing measure continues to tug the concept of the public interest into the pragmatist's corner.

Of course, while many of us have the luxury of speculating about what influences the public interest and what it *should* be, there are several thousand people who help define it in everyday practice—the broadcasters, their managers, programmers, newspersons, and others. They are at the center of all the influences—government regulations, the public interest, local needs, economic success, the ratings, individual audience member's complaints and compliments, and so on. Here lies one of our system's greatest strengths. Each broadcaster must assess all these influences and set priorities in terms of the locale in which he or she operates. Local audiences and their needs, tastes, and values will determine to a great degree the success or failure of programming decisions. Given the differences that make each locale unique in so many ways, the result is a diversity of programming, especially considering the media competition in American communities. Certainly one could argue that the new technology of delivery (satellites music networks, electronic newsgathering innovations, increased network services, and others) is bringing more standardization and "sameness" to our content, but the essence of the system remains locally based. Continued developments such as potential direct satellite-to-home transmissions, increasing importation by cable of alternative programming, and so on may diminish the local flavor of "the public interest" in the practitioner's mind, some sources would argue.

While the public interest has connoted noble values and goals for many, it has also served as a strategic banner in which numerous opportunists have wrapped their special causes. After all, asserting that one's own interests are synonymous with the greater public good is a rhetorical technique dating back to Aristotle's time! It's not our purpose here to make value judgments about the merit of various special interest groups, or to provide a history lesson on all the attempts made to amend in one way or another the statutory or regulatory conceptions of the public interest. Rather, the attempt in this essay is to point out that the evolution of special interest initiatives— some successful, some not—have influenced the working interpretations of the concept rather significantly.

One prime example involves the incumbent office-holders who have over the years voted themselves special access and reduced advertising rates in the name of the public interest by amending the Communications Act.

Special interests have continually sought free access to broadcast airtime, and others have suggested that various "cause" groups have percentages of time allotted to them by statute or regulation. During the long debate over license renewal standards (What criteria shall govern whether a station has served the public interest?) a parade of witnesses argued that various quantitative guidelines (guaranteeing their programming be aired) would be one strong measure of whether or not a station had served "the public" well.

Most readers well understand that key political decision makers have great influence over various standards of service in the public interest. For example, chairmen of the U.S. House and Senate Communications subcommittees, Appropriations Committees, administration officials, and FCC chairmen have all had much direct impact on policy through specific actions and proposals.

What is interesting to observe is the vast influence their *indirect* actions, statements, and personal comments have had as well. One of the most colorful was U.S. Senate Communications Chair John Pastore (D.-R.I.) whose flailings, speeches, and admonitions had significant influence on the communication policy-making agenda across the board. U.S. House Communications Subcommittee Chair Lionel Van Deerlin (D.-Calif.) shook up the industry and its regulators for over two years with his calls for a "rewrite" of the "ancient" Communications Act, though actual legislation never emerged. FCC chairmen have had similar impact. How many times have we heard quoted FCC Chairman Newton Minow's blast at TV as a "wasteland"? And a subsequent FCC chair, Mark Fowler, created controversy (and some Capitol Hill backlash in both parties) with his tenacious but earnest calls for total deregulation of the communications industry. A key to his concept of the public interest was for broadcasters to operate with full First Amendment freedoms. Such policy-makers have significant influence in setting the agenda, the tone, the philosophical context, targeting criticism . . . all in addition to taking direct action.

By no means is this brief discussion of various sets of influences comprehensive, but hopefully it helps stimulate further analysis. While as analysts of the public interest we can speculate what influences shape this concept, it's productive as well to grapple with forming our own conception of what it means to meet this elusive standard. The following are some of the elements this writer would identify as essential to a broadcaster serving the public interest. How closely do they match your own?

- Operating with an overall commitment to serving the community in a way that goes beyond one's self-interest. The realities of staying economically viable have been discussed, and that essential is our system. Concurrently, it seems that broadcasters have an obligation—which most fulfill admirably—to serve unique community needs with programming.

- Practicing the philosophy of "reinvesting" in one's own station to the extent possible to insure high quality performance over the long term and avoid rapid ownership turnovers.

- Active participation of station management and staff in community organizations, problem solving, and citizen boards. Success in broadcasting will to a growing degree depend upon real and effective daily integration with one's community in a personal way. No longer can a good broadcaster well serve an audience while lacking meaningful contact with their daily lives.

- Realizing that broadcasting is not only a tremendous medium for entertainment—of which we can be proud—but also must provide a diversity of news, education, and information in *innovative* formats.

- Insuring that stations and systems of broadcasting not only reflect the uniqueness of our communities, but through national networks and programming provide regional and national views of life. Indeed, broadcasting today is the prime means through which we view cultures beyond our own.

- While compliance with existing law and regulation is essential, this does not preclude opposing on a personal policy basis unneeded government intrusion. Too many broadcasters continue to avoid an active role in lobbying personally for policies that would enhance their ability to serve. It is also the industry's responsibility to fight aggressively government attempts to erode our freedoms and use our advertising and programming as scapegoats for societal problems.

In researching out our own goals of service in the public interest, it may be helpful as well to note what such service does not include. Here's a beginning, again from a personal perspective.

- A strength of our system is that it's composed for the most part of independent, intelligent people making decisions about programming in response to audiences served. Broadcasting should never function as a common carrier in any way, "passing through" mandated content.

- While we need maximum freedom for our journalists to operate effectively, broadcasting in the public interest does not mean that news should operate without accountability to the values of balance, accuracy, attribution, and perspective. Aggressiveness in reporting without adherence to a sense of responsibility has no business in journalism. Our credibility as broadcasters operating in the public interest suffers greatly when newspeople do not adhere to these professional values.

- Serving the public interest does not mean being sychophants for the loudest critics, be they clients, office holders, or special interests. Nor does it mean imitation of competitors' successful formats, storylines, or whatever. Within our economic resources broadcasting should *innovate* as well as mirror.

Hopefully, this discussion has demonstrated that many factors influence "the public interest," its definition and application. This concept is basically a guide that continues to evolve, and through this evolutionary process, reflect the diversity of those served.

Notes

1. Bernard C. Hennessy, *Public Opinion* (Belmont, Calif.: Wadsworth Publishing Company, Inc., 1965), 275.

7

SERVING PUBLIC
INTEREST

In this careful analysis of the concept of public interest, Ted Snider points out that the authors of the 1927 and 1934 federal acts to regulate broadcasting never intended to grant public ownership of the airwaves because frequencies hold "no intrinsic value." While the government may have the right to regulate the spectrum, the gist of his argument is that Congress has simply ignored the First Amendment to thrust upon the broadcasters onerous regulations governing what they can broadcast. Such regulation has been justified on the grounds of spectrum scarcity even though broadcasters occupy only a small fraction of the whole frequency spectrum, and despite the fact that the rest of the spectrum users are held accountable by the government only for their record of technical use. As a result, the broadcaster has been made a "second-class citizen."

Until Congress takes clear steps to free the broadcaster from the shackles of program regulation, to allow the programming the same rights that exist for other forms of communication under the First Amendment, the free marketplace of ideas will never be totally free. The concept of scarcity that began the process of federal regulation no longer justifies stringent regulation of broadcast programming, if it ever did. It is sufficient to have the government assure that the signal received is clear and free of interference. Let the broadcaster decide what should be programmed, serving the public in a competitive market, free of federal intimidation.

About the Author

Ted L. Snider received a B.A. degree in 1949 and an M.A. in 1950 from Baylor University with a major in radio broadcasting. In 1950, he also completed the UCLA-NBC-TV Television Institute in Hollywood. He served in the Marine Corps during the Korean War and is now a retired captain in the U.S. Naval Reserve.

He began his broadcasting career as a radio announcer, then held the following positions (in chronological order): radio time salesman, television announcer, TV program director, TV time salesman, TV station manager, radio station manager, radio station owner. He has worked for KAND (Corsicana, Texas), KWTX and WACO (Waco, Texas), KFBM-TV (San Diego, California), KOAT-TV (Albuquerque, New Mexico), WTCN-TV (Minneapolis, Minnesota), KBST (Big Spring, Texas), and KPAY (Little Rock, Arkansas). He is the owner of KARN and KKYK in Little Rock, the Arkansas Radio Network, MUZAK, and Snider Communications Corporation (Snider Telecom).

His activities in the National Association of Broadcasters include: speaker, NAB National Convention (1976); NAB Board of Directors (1981–1987); vice chairman (1984); chairman (1985) of the NAB Radio Board and member of the Executive Committee (1983–1987); NAB Joint Board chairman (1985–1987).

He has also served the Arkansas Broadcasters Association on the Board of Directors (1970–1973, 1981–1987), and as president (1974). He was speaker, RAB Management Conference (1965, 1972); president, AP Broadcasters of Arkansas (1971), and a member of the Executive Committee, NBC Affiliates (1969–1976). He has been involved in many civic organizations in California and Arkansas.

Serving the Public Interest: Voluntarily or by Government Mandate?

TED L. SNIDER

In the nation's Capitol the phrase "in the public interest" is bandied about in all sorts of contexts. It is a symbolic phrase that has special meaning in broadcasting. Another phrase frequently used is "public trusteeship." Too often these phrases are mentioned without an understanding of their basic meanings. Is there a difference between "public trusteeship" and "in the public interest"? Is there a linkage? How does the answer to this question affect broadcasters? It affects the very foundation of our business—our license to broadcast. First a couple of definitions:

TRUSTEE: One who manages (looks after) the property of another for another's benefit.

TRUSTEESHIP: The act of managing the property or affairs of another.

Public trusteeship implies the management of property or affairs of the public for the public's benefit. "In the public interest" means doing good for the public but not necessarily involving any public ownership.

Let's take a close look at the concept of public trusteeship. Exactly what is it? Trusteeship involves *management* and *ownership*. Public trusteeship of the airways implies the management of the airways for the public's benefit, which in turn implies that the airways are *owned* by the public.

Ownership means holding title to something of value. But what is the intrinsic value of the airways or the ether? Some analogies may be useful here.

Public ownership of highways, for example, involves something purchased: material, land, labor, maintenance, and repair. The same is true for public ownership of certain utilities, such as municipal water and electricity. The highways and utilities, as well as the public buildings, monuments and museums all have intrinsic value, and, therefore, ownership is meaningful. They fall in one particular category: *accessible and ownable*. Certain rules and regulations are required for their use so as to maintain order, avoid chaos, and promote preservation.

There is another category: accessible but *not* ownable. Included in this category are the passageways through which something travels: the seas, the air and skies, "outer space," and the electromagnetic airwaves or ether. These are different in that they cannot be created, taken title to or owned, or bought and sold. They have no intrinsic value, yet they can be used for the good of humankind when, and only when, humankind learns how to use them. It is only the means and the knowledge that enable people to make use of this nonownable category. The means and the knowledge have value—they *can* be owned, bought, and sold. The means include the ships that ply the seas, the planes that fly through the air, the satellites that travel in outer space, and the transmitters and associated equipment that generate and transmit information, sound, and pictures through the ether. The means require investment and knowledge. While the means are ownable, the passageways are not. These means can be worn out, used up, or become outdated. But use of the ether in no ways uses it up, deteriorates it, or damages it. It doesn't have to be replenished, regenerated, or repaired. Its life is limitless.

Both categories—accessible and ownable, and accessible but not ownable—are similar in that rules and regulations are necessary to maintain order. As for the accessible but not ownable category, their regulations include the international rules of the road employed on the high seas, airline regulations recognized around the world, international agreements on orbital positioning of satellites, and international technical agreements to maintain order in the ether. Society recognizes the necessity of these regulations. So do the users.

What does this have to do with broadcasters? Just this: Passageways such as the ether (the so-called "public airways") are not ownable. The public does *not own* them and cannot hold title to them because they have no intrinsic value. Research by the Library of Congress' Congressional Research Service, NAB attorneys, and various legal scholars has shown that the authors of the Radio Act of 1927 and The Communications Act of 1934 never intended that the public owns the airwaves. Government has only the right to regulate.

Ships, planes, satellites, and transmitters are licensed in order to maintain accountability. In the United States they are owned and operated commercially. All shipping companies, airlines, satellite owners, and users of the electromagnetic spectrum—except broadcasters—are treated the same. Furthermore, all spectrum licensees are required to operate "in the public interest, necessity and convenience." Somehow, Congress singled out broadcasters, expanded "operate" to "operate and program," and decreed that broadcasters were "trustees of the public airways" and were licensed to "operate *and program* in the public interest, necessity and convenience." Only broadcast licensees were subjected to this programming requirement. The explanation was spectrum scarcity, the laws of physics—it is possible for only one transmitter to use the same frequency in the same area at the same time. While this is true of landing slots, docking berths, orbit slots, and all other communications frequencies, only broadcasters are saddled with the programming content public interest standard.

Broadcasters are in the business of communicating with the public through their programming. So are newspapers, magazines, signs, direct mailers, and skywriters. But none of them is burdened with a *content* public interest standard. Historically, spectrum scarcity is the reason given for treating broadcasters differently. Realistically, however, the laws of economics are every bit as restrictive as the laws of physics. Indeed, the laws of economics have forced the closure of hundreds of newspapers and periodicals. Congress has recognized economic scarcity by passing the Newspaper Preservation Act, which allows newspapers to share physical facilities. Zoning laws have forced the removal of signs. There are limited orbital slots. The U.S. Postal Service has definite restrictions on direct mail; otherwise it simply would be unable to handle the volume. And skywriters are a vanishing breed.

Then there is the matter of length of licenses, challenges, and renewals. The owners of ships, airlines, satellites, signs, as well as the users of nonbroadcast spectrum have their licenses for as long as they do not violate technical regulations. There are no content regulations. No matter who else may want those landing slots, docking berths, sign sites, orbital slots, or communications frequencies, they are available only through purchase. There are no renewals, proceedings, challenges to the licenses or slots by others who want them, or content public interest standards by which to be challenged.

Why are broadcasters singled out and saddled with a programming content public interest standard by which they live or die? Why are broadcasters singled out for bans on the advertising of cigarettes, smokeless tobacco advertising, and lotteries? Why are broadcasters singled out for price controls on political advertising, for equal time requirements (Section 315, Fairness Doctrine), and the requirement to treat issues of "public importance"? Very simply, it's because Congress, in violation of the First Amendment, decided to treat broadcasters as second-class citizens. How long are we going to sit still for this?

Broadcasters are specifically regulated by only two entities: the Federal Communications Commission and the Congress. The FCC has only recently recognized that broadcasters have long been sorely discriminated against, and it has initiated an era of deregulation. The FCC, however, is limited to repealing its *own* regulations. It cannot repeal any of the provisions of the Communications Act. As a result, broadcasters are left with the Fairness Doctrine—a questionable policy—Section 315, license renewals, and license challenges (comparative renewals). Yet broadcasters use only a small part of the vast frequency spectrum. No other users of the spectrum face these critical threats. Why has Congress singled out broadcasters?

The answers range from the honest convictions of dedicated public officials to the belief of others that control of broadcasting will improve their chances of reelection. It's the only remaining public communications medium over which (by means of content regulation) the government has the power of life or death. The government doesn't have this power over newspapers, magazines, direct mail, signs, or, just recently, cable—only broadcasting. And this is in spite of the fact that the First Amendment says in no uncertain terms that "Congress shall make no law ... abridging the freedom of speech or of the press...."

The English kept their thumbs on the Colonies. The Colonists recognized this taxation without representation was patently unfair, and the American Revolution set it right. They had no court to turn to, but they would not tolerate unfairness. In their unusual wisdom, the colonists wrote the Constitution and the Bill of Rights, quickly adding the First Amendment granting freedom of speech, which everyone has enjoyed in this country for over 200 years—that is, everyone except broadcasters!

There are those in Congress in key positions who insist on keeping their thumbs on broadcasters' First Amendment rights. In their view, our founding fathers, with quill pens in hand, had written these words: "Congress shall make no law abridging freedom of speech or of the press except, of course, if the law pertains to regulation of radio and television broadcasters." With a few, perhaps it's the jealousy of power, the insistence on control. With others, it may be simply a misguided notion of public trusteeship, born out of an ignorance of the facts.

Some Congressmen say broadcasters are special. Because broadcasters use the so-called "public airways," they say we have a special obligation to program "in the public interest" by adhering to a broadly worded "public interest standard." We *are* special but no more so than many other types of businesses. Hospitals are special. They have an obligation to care for human lives. Do they have program content restrictions? No—only technical operating standards. And bankers have a special fiduciary responsibility but no programming content—only technical operating standards and accountability. Also, banks have limited licenses or charters. And doctors—are they special? Doctors have awesome responsibilities—often a matter of life or death—but no "public interest standard" is applied over and above their ethical and operating standards. Add to this restaurants (sanitary standards), food and drug manufacturers (health standards), airlines (safety standards), and utilities.

These businesses and professions have special obligations to the public—and most have limited permits—but no content regulation. Only broadcasters are burdened with the "public interest standard" over and above technical operating requirements. Yet all these other businesses and professions must be licensed and regulated, even as broadcasters are. So why do license renewals depend on a finding by the FCC that our stations' program content meet some "public interest standard"? These other businesses and professions operate in "the public interest" without a governmentally mandated public interest standard requirement for license renewal. They operate in "the public interest"—not because the government requires it but because it is good business. But there are those who suggest legislating "good works." That is like legislating morals! It doesn't make any sense.

Broadcasters have always operated in the public interest and been doers of good. They always will because they want their communities to be better places in which to live. Serving others is a noble and gratifying endeavor. It is simply good business to be responsible to their constituencies. It's also good for department stores, restaurants, banks, and plumbing concerns. None needs the government to legislate good works. We do well by doing good. It's a law of good business. There are ample laws governing criminal behavior, antitrust and discrimination in business, pornography, etc. Broadcasters don't need additional statutes that say, in effect, "meet the government's programming standards or we'll put you out of business." As long as Congress can control program content in broadcasting, it can mandate what broadcasters can advertise, charge, and program. It can invoke its will on political advertising, news programming, and product advertising. And if it doesn't like what broadcasters program, it can impose sanctions, intimidate, and cancel licenses.

There are broadcasters who are comfortable with program content regulation because it gives them guidelines for keeping their licenses. They endorse a standard, referred to as the public interest standard, by which they can be measured and, if they measure up, can stay in business by fending off challenges and petitions to deny. But no other mass communications medium lives under such a sword of Damocles. Broadcasters must "make points" by adhering to a legislated public interest standard in order to "get credit," which might be needed as an offset in case of a challenge to their license or a competing application. And that is probably true as long as Congress allows comparative renewals based on programming content and licenses are not routinely renewed subject only to adherence to technical regulations.

Broadcasters are bound and trusted by the personal philosophies of a few congressmen in key chairmanships. These congressmen are determined to hold broadcasters hostage. And broadcasters are forced to forgo their First Amendment rights because only by submitting to a legislated public interest standard can they "make points" by which to stave off a threat to their licenses in a comparative renewal proceeding.

Broadcasters are second class citizens in the business community. They can never enjoy full freedom of speech until Congress passes a law that eliminates comparative renewal based on programming content. Passage of such a law should be the number-one priority of free, over-the-air broadcasters. The comparative renewal process is an abomination that allows a challenge to a license based on programming content promises. We broadcasters deserve license renewals like all non-broadcast users of the spectrum when we adhere to technical standards. Elimination of the comparative renewal is also a way to stop the strike application, which many times is a legalized form of extortion having nothing to do with the public interest. We must not pay too high a price— and codifying the public interest standard and the Fairness Doctrine is too high.

Comparative renewal proceedings involve contests between businessmen. They have nothing to do with the public's rights. The public still has the right to petition or complain, just as they do with other licensed businesses.

The airways are not, nor can they be, owned by the public. Broadcasters are not public trustees. Indeed we do not have any more special obligation to the public than other types of businesses that are licensed. We do not deserve to be burdened with a "public interest" over and above technical operating standards in order to get our licenses renewed or to eliminate comparative renewal. It is unfair that we, and only we, are forced to operate under an unceasing threat by challengers who want to put us out of business—or the government, which wants to control us by denying our First Amendment rights.

For too long we've allowed "Big Brother" to control us. For too long we've meekly accepted unfair treatment and even outright discrimination. We have a case, and we need to make it. We need to stand up and speak for ourselves. If we don't, who will?

8

CENSORSHIP AND PUBLIC INTEREST

While William O'Shaughnessy recognizes that the airwaves belong to the people, he expresses concern that the First Amendment is ignored, indeed violated, when the FCC objects to program content. Despite the fact that there may be controversy over what is acceptable proper broadcasting, federal intervention is an unacceptable solution. The broadcaster, and ultimately those who are served by the broadcaster, must be the arbiters of what is acceptable. The First Amendment was designed to protect—and should protect—against "intolerable intrusions" by federal regulators.

The protection guaranteed by the First Amendment applies as much to the broadcasting industry as to any other form of mass communication. While this protection started with the printed word, it is just as applicable to the invisible frequencies, which, despite the early technological limitations used to justify federal legislation, are now so pervasive that virtually everywhere one can receive a variety of radio and television programs via cable, satellite, VCR, and over the air.

So why the continued federal preoccupation with program content? Those who look to the federal government to regulate objectionable material ignore a basic tenet of personal freedom that has served this country well. Federal censorship can never be the answer, no matter how tempting and easy that prospect might seem. The right and responsibility for content control lies with the broadcaster who must ultimately answer to the public in order to prosper, and with the public who has the power to hold the broadcaster accountable.

About the Author

William O'Shaughnessy is president and chief executive officer of WVOX-AM in Westchester, New York, a station that the *Wall Street Journal* has described as "the quintessential community radio station in America," and WRTN-FM, a jazz-swing station. He served as president of the New York State Broadcasters Association and as a director of the National Association of Broadcasters.

O'Shaughnessy serves as his stations' editorial director. He has been a recipient of the Radio-Television News Directors (RTNDA) Award from Indiana University for "The Outstanding Editorials in the U.S. and Canada." He has also received the Communications Medal from the Archdiocese of New York; the Crystal Prism Award from the American Advertising Federation; the George Washington Medal from the Freedoms Foundation at Valley Forge; and the Abraham Lincoln Merit Award from the Southern Baptist Radio-TV Commission.

He serves as director of the Archdiocese of New York Substance Abuse Ministry; as president of the State Club, Inc., a forum for educators, academics, business leaders, and public servants, which encourages and fosters good government, and holds membership in the International Radio-Television Society and the Broadcast Pioneers. He was founder and former chairman of the New York Market Radio Broadcasters Association (NYMRAD), and founder of the Nelson A. Rockefeller Minority Internship Program (NYSBA).

Broadcasting and Censorship: Government's Intrusion and Public Interest

WILLIAM O'SHAUGHNESSY

My Westchester neighbor, Julian Goodman (a former chairman of NBC), once observed that we broadcasters have an "awesome trust." It is a lovely and graceful phrase. We struggle and we churn about this, and we worry about recent actions of the FCC and the Parents Music Resource Center (PMRC).

Broadcasters are permittees and trustees, and we have a fiduciary relationship to the airwaves which rightly and properly belong to the people of this country. Many, perhaps even most, of us believe that a radio station achieves its highest calling when it resembles a platform, a forum, a soapbox for the expression of many different viewpoints. And even in this high-tech, speeded-up, electronic age free, over-the-air radio is still the medium closest to the people. We proudly point to its ability to deliver upscale, affluent listeners, but radio is also the intimate, personal companion of the poor, the misunderstood, and the disenfranchised. Therein lies its potential—and its greatness.

In California last month, Mario Cuomo, the gifted and sensitive governor of New York, said: "Broadcasters have the power to amplify the goodness in any community . . . and to make us sweeter than we are." We can thus aspire to be more than performers or entertainers. And a radio station *can* be something more than a jukebox.

And so we speak out on controversial issues and try to provide leadership in our community. The First Amendment is very impor-

This essay is based on an Op Ed Commentary delivered over WRTN and WVOX on October 1, 1987.

tant, almost sacred. We will fight anyone who would dare stifle one of our newscasts or editorial pronouncements. I'm not sure that the popular songs of our day and the public utterances of disc jockeys and talk-shows hosts might not deserve the same sensitivity and protection and consideration as our own majestic editorial declarations, no matter how gross, no matter how clumsy, no matter how outrageous.

I come from a place in the East where once lived an obscure printer called Zenger, John Peter Zenger. He risked all to be able to rage against the despotic governor. He chose to do this with his pen and with a printing press. But what of the modern songwriter...the bard...the poet...the minstrel...of the day who talks of his demons and the things which oppress him, whether that song is a polemic, a political statement, or just a lonely cry for understanding?

And what of the irreverent disc jockey or talk-show host struggling to expose difficult truths or merely to poke fun at all our pretensions? Our program talent, struggling to communicate in the vernacular and with the currency of the day in all their occasional grossness and clumsiness and in all their lack of grace and finesse and style, deserve to be protected from the prevailing attitudes of Federal bureaucrats and self-anointed censors in every instance.

They deserve the opportunity to be rejected only by the broadcaster functioning in our role as fudiciary and trustee or only by those people we serve and with whom we reside as citizens and neighbors whose decency and goodness and perception *we must trust.*

Clearly, recent actions of the FCC and the PMRC represent *intolerable intrusions* into program content. The broadcasts for which Pacifica or Howard Stern stand accused may have been indecent or obscene. That judgment, however, should be left to the broadcaster and thus to the viewer or listener who should be able, in this republic, to exercise the ultimate and only permissible censorship by tuning out material which may be offensive to his or her eye or ear or sensibilities.

As a result of the commission's recent actions, the whole profession, the whole "industry," if you prefer, is now at risk and at peril forever. For as it now stands: *anything* can be held to be indecent by three individuals, three bureaucrats, sitting on the commission. We *cannot* relax these principles now for strategic or political reasons (an argument we heard in the effort by Congress to codify Fairness [doctrine]). We can't choose our fights based on popular support...or a lack of votes...or the prevailing mood of the Congress...or in an effort to curry favor with the Washington Establishment or the current administration.

I acknowledge my belief in the existence of Evil which is to be fought in every way, on a daily basis, in our own *personal* lives. But as broadcasters and as citizens and as passionate believers in the Constitution whose birthday we proclaim and celebrate in gratitude, we have to take our stand with the raucous . . . and the gross . . . and the clumsy . . . and the sensational.

In Elizabethan times the language was much broader. The vernacular included words we would not accept in daily usage or in the media. But restricting language is only possible in a totalitarian atmosphere. It was possible in Germany. It is possible in Bulgaria. It is possible today in Cuba. It is possible where one mode of communication predominates.

There is a feeling abroad in the land that community standards differ by market size or geography. But as a result of our "wired nation" and the modern technology of cable and satellites and networks and super stations, *we are all one* . . . and many feel that purveyors of filth should be driven from our ranks *at any cost*. But I'm not willing to pay the price. Our disagreement is on the *choice of referee*. We believe the American people should blow the whistle and control the clock . . . by tuning us out . . . and that the institution established by the people for social policy disputes—the courts—should handle any protests beyond that.

I make a living playing the songs of Fred Astaire . . . and Mabel Mercer . . . and Bobby Short. I don't even understand most of the songs on today's hit parade. But I'm persuaded they deserve respect and sensitivity from us. A song is like an eyewitness report. The writers of those songs write of the daily life in America, the daily passions of our countrymen, the milieu in which they live. In any society there is a fine line of taste which constantly changes. The populace redraws it every season. And we can't stop it.

What is the difference betweeen a suggestive lyric and a dirty lyric? What is the difference between prurient and risque? I'm afraid that the scraggly haired, unshaven songwriter of gross, clumsy, prurient—even vulgar—lyrics has to be treated with the same protection and sensitivity we now give, in retrospect, and with great affection, to Cole Porter or Johnny Mercer or Johnny Burke. Puritan America would not let us use the word "hell" on radio for many years. Indeed, and somewhat ironically, the word "virgin" was considered unacceptable for a good long time. But to assume that popular songs can be apart from the vernacular itself is a mistake.

The Parents Music Resource Center, Morality in Media, and other censors careening around Washington want a world which is uncomplicated . . . without pain for their children . . . not obscene . . . and not profane.

But the hard, real truth is that their children, *our* children, in their private lives, are meeting the very influences we are trying to restrict. Indeed, if you've ever debriefed a child on return from summer camp ... you will realize that children make up their own songs which are a lot *worse* than those on the radio!

I'm afraid we have a great fear of *what we already know*. Those who fight pornography know the *meanings* of the words. They have used and *lived* them. But nothing has happened to them. They are upstanding and respectable. Because nothing takes the place of an *honest home*.

We are concerned about children, our most precious resource. They are of us. They are ours. But the only thing we can hope for is that what we give them at home will prevail and carry them through life. If parents give our children the right kind of vehicle, those kids will float on any kind of debris. The censors and the blue noses can't, however, get rid of the debris. It's always been there. It's part of the landscape. It's called life.

The PMRC and the Brad Curls want the atmosphere and the milieu of their homes to prevail in society at large. But that wonderful, warm, stable, secure atmopshere in Albert and Tipper Gore's home is not the same as the atmosphere or milieu which confronts a ghetto kid in Harlem ... or the farm boy in Bismarck ... or a beach boy in Berkeley ... or even an oil-rig worker in Texas. It is all different.

Nothing "encourages" people to sin or change history. Songs are *signs ... banners*. They do not make history. Without the banner, the parade will go on. And which words are really obscene? Is "fuck" really worse than "nigger" and "kike"? Which is *ultimately* more obscene and indecent?

The Fundamentalists, who have relentlessly lobbied Congress and recent appointees to the FCC, have probably forgotten that Jesus of Nazareth showed great compassion for prostitutes and other sinners against "the flesh" ... while reserving His greatest disapproaval for the self-righteous, the hypocrites, the chief priests, elders and magistrates of the day.

And so we are often left with only vulgarity ... and grossness ... and some fragile notions about something called Free Speech.

We have always had terrible examples to defend.

IN THE
MARKETPLACE

9

PUBLIC INTEREST
AND LOCAL
IDENTITY

Whatever can be said about the legal or social implications of the concept of public interest, it finally boils down to how the individual station interacts with the community. In the accompanying article, Wayne Vriesman specifically details how WGN has created a strong identity in Chicago through a variety of individual efforts. As he describes it, WGN offers "public service in action." Its success is measured specifically in dollars raised, in canned food collected, in involving the community as partners in voluntary activities. The activities he writes about have served to make WGN a civic leader.

Like many other broadcast stations across the United States, WGN has become a successful business enterprise because it used its access to the spectrum to benefit the local community in many ways, none of which have been proscribed by federal regulation. WGN's record of working with the community illustrates how well a station can do if it is willing to serve the public interest well, not just in terms of editorials, news coverage, or investigative reporting (which are important), but as an involved partner.

It did not take federal legislation to force WGN into its commitment to Chicago. Good business sense made it obvious that to do well against strong competition, the broadcaster has to see the community marketplace as more than a mere source of revenue. Public interest requires community involvement because social commitment is good business.

About the Author

Wayne R. Vriesman was named vice president of Tribune Radio Group, Chicago, on October 1, 1987. In this position he has supervision of radio stations in New York City; Bridgeport, Connecticut; Chicago, Illinois; and Sacramento, California.

He joined WGN, Chicago, in 1960 as a news writer, after earning a B.A. degree from Hope College and a master's degree in journalism from Northwestern University. He was promoted to news producer for WGN-TV and the following year was named night news editor for radio and television. He transferred to WGN Continental's Denver station in 1966 to head the news operation of KWGN-TV. In 1973, he was elected a vice president of WGN of Colorado, Inc., and a year later was named a director of that company.

In January 1977 he returned to Chicago as news director for WGN Radio and Television, and was elected a vice president of WGN in May of that year. He was named station manager of WGN Radio in July 1978.

From December 1976 to December 1977, Vriesman served as national president of the Radio and Television News Directors Association (RTNDA). He is currently serving as president of the Illinois Broadcasters Association.

WGN Radio: Public Interest Means Local Identity

WAYNE R. VRIESMAN

"How does WGN do it?" That question, or one like it, is asked quite often, mostly by other broadcasters. What they want to know is how WGN has fought the virtual tidal wave of FM and stayed a dominant Number One in the Chicago market to boot.

Our answer is simple: WGN *is* Chicago.

That might seem like a cliché or a bit of braggadocia. But it's true. Our call letters are among the best known in the nation and certainly the best known in this market. They denote service, quality, and stability. That's why WGN is Chicago. We serve the Chicago metropolitan area with quality news, sports, and entertainment that reflects its needs and desires, and we've done it for a long time.

Chicagoans want to know what's going on in their world—not all the news, but the important news—and we tell them. We're not locked into a formula of two minutes of news at forty after the hour. We do schedule newscasts, but the news of the day is a large part of a program flow.

But, that's just part of it. It's also the mix and personality that helps us serve so many people. It's a little bit of this and a little bit of that. It's like what they used to say about Chicago's weather: If you don't like it, wait a little while and you'll get something different.

It all adds up to serving the community. There's news and information—with special traffic, weather, business, and sports reports during drive time—and there are other elements. We have regular theater, film, and music reviews—what's happening on the Chicago scene. We cover a broad range of public events and issues in talk shows. Some of our "Talkers" use a little music and, yes, we have two or three music programs weekly.

Then, there's the frosting on the cake: play-by-play sports! We carry the games most Chicagoans want to hear: Chicago Bears and Notre Dame football, Chicago Cubs baseball, and DePaul and Notre Dame basketball.

What we do isn't cheap. In fact, it costs us a lot of money. But the quality we're buying tells, and the old saying is quite true. "It takes money to make money."

We have a group of program hosts who are among the best in the country, paid accordingly, and each provided with a producer—not just a phone screener, but a producer—to contribute to that overall quality. We have a large news staff, a department of play-by-play people and sports reporters. We do a lot of remotes, not just play-by-play, so the folks out there can see us doing what we do best. And yes, we have a one-hour farm show at noon. How's that for service?

What we do has become an important part of Chicago's everyday life. It's public service in action. We do it well. We do it profitably. And we have fun doing it.

"Charity," we've been told, "begins at home." In our home, charity is a very important thing, both on and off the air.

On-air support of special projects in 1986 raised cash contributions of more than $1.3 million for the *Neediest Children's Fund*, approximately $60 thousand for the *Good Neighbor Food Drive*, $100 thousand for the Chicago Division of the American Cancer Society, and about $75 thousand for the Salvation Army in Chicago.

In addition, WGN Radio made direct cash contributions, amounting to more than $40 thousand, to a wide variety of local charities. The value of programming and time devoted to the *Neediest Children's Fund* is valued at $120,000, while the value of all other public service announcements aired in 1986 is placed at $316,500. Finally, WGN Radio spent in excess of $20,000 to provide space, equipment, and support services for the Chicago Branch of Call for Action. The rest of this article will be devoted to more specific details about how WGN carries out its public-interest commitment to Chicago.

The Good Neighbor Food Drive

To insomniacs and to others who just like to listen to radio in the wee, small hours of the morning, overnight personality Ed Schwartz is known as "Chicago Ed." It's a name he has earned. He is as "Chicago" as anyone can be.

Being a night watcher and being on the other end of the mike—and the telephone—Ed has been a touch-point for all-night Chicago for years. At the turn of the decade, Ed became aware through the calls he was receiving that, while most of us were at least "getting along," more of us were going hungry.

Ed wanted to help. He got together with the leadership of the Church Federation of Metropolitan Chicago, an agency well aware of hunger and already trying to do something about it. Ed volunteered to use his microphone and WGN Radio's reach to join the campaign. Organization was not simple. But two weeks before Christmas in 1982, with the help of hundreds of volunteers and the support of dozens of companies and public and private agencies, "Chicago Ed" hosted the city's largest and longest food drive. In the bitter cold, Ed broadcast from outside the WGN studios, then on the city's northwest side, describing the continuous line of cars entering the parking lot, each carrying a bag or box of groceries. When Christmas came, there still were hungry people in Chicago, but their number had been diminished.

The "cast" for the remote included dozens of public figures—celebrities from politics, sports, and the entertainment world—and a lot of other folks who just came by to help the less fortunate. The 1986 food drive, the biggest ever, was held in front of the city's official Christmas tree at the Richard J. Daley Plaza in the heart of the city.

When it was all over, after nine hours, more than a quarter of a million pounds of food had been collected, and more came later. Cash contributions of nearly $60,000 enabled the Church Federation to buy more food, valued at three times that amount. The collection netted more than twice the food it brought in during the previous drive. Over the air, it sounded like "a good night's work." There is no way to measure the many nights'—and days'—work, both by a few dozen WGN Radio staffers and hundreds of others who made it possible. But it was worth it!

Neediest Children's Fund

Most communities have some project in which all media cooperate, such as the annual United Way Campaign. Chicago's very own such project is the Neediest Children's Christmas Fund.

The role of WGN, through the on-air efforts of Wally Phillips as a participant as long ago as 1975, is unique. Checks totaling more than $1.3 *million* were sent to Wally in 1986. That accounted for more than 40% of the total contributions to this cause.

More and more has been contributed each year. Often what might have been spent on an office Christmas party, or what a group of youngsters might have collected for a gift for their teacher, is sent to Wally for the kids.

When the fund began, it was designed to provide Christmas toys to youngsters whose families were on welfare, children who would have received nothing from Santa otherwise. As more money was raised, the fund was able to help entire families. Wally chose, however, to keep his collections for the kids.

Another element in this project is gifts from clients and others. These items often are auctioned to benefit the fund. And in January of each year, all the letters or envelopes which brought the checks are put into a huge drum for a daily prize drawing. Illinois Governor Jim Thompson, Chicago Mayors Harold Washington and Jane Byrne, Bears running back Walter Payton, and other celebrities do the drawing on a daily basis until all the prizes are gone. By then, it's time to begin the drive for next Christmas.

Bob Rings the Bell

Morning man Bob Collins is a supporter of the Salvation Army off the air as well as on. In addition to raising $75,000 directly last year, Bob and his morning crew make public appearances for the Army and always spend some time "ringing the bell" next to a kettle outside a major department store.

The *Chicago Sun-Times* recently held a popularity contest to "pick Chicago's favorite morning disc jockey." Bob Collins won, of course. The prize was one full-page ad each month for a year. That's a great temptation for a jock and his station. How to use that full-page a month presented no problem for Bob Collins. He used it as a community calendar, open to any not-for-profit organization to list its upcoming activities.

Allstar Sport Fishing Tournament

For the third consecutive year, the host of WGN Radio's "Great Outdoors," Bill Cullerton, was the moving force behind this event which raised $100,000 for the American Cancer Society. In addition to the on-air support provided by Bill on his own program, fishing celebrities Bob Collins in morning drive and Paul Brian in mid-day, promoted the event heavily.

Other Charity Involvement

Most of the other personalities on WGN Radio also are involved in special projects, both on and off the air. Roy Leonard is a charter member and past president of the Red Cloud Association, funding a range of programs for American Indians. Spike O'Dell has lent his support to the Special Olympics. Paul Brian is an active member of the Shriners, doing more for that organization off the air than on, and what he does on the air is substantial. Sports Director Chuck Swirsky serves on the Board of Directors of the Brian Piccolo (cancer research) Foundation and is active with Big Brothers/Big Sisters. Steve King and Johnnie Putman—off the air Mr. and Mrs.—are active with the Les Turner ALS Foundation and the Muscular Dystrophy Association.

Through our thirty-year association with the Chicago Cubs, we play an active role in Cubs Care, which holds an auction and dinner each year for the cancer research facility at Northwestern Memorial Hospital. WGN sponsors the annual golf tournament of Chicago Baseball Charities and participates in the benefit activities of the Chicago Bears. In addition, the station sponsored the trip of a team of bright Illinois teenagers who represented this state in the Academic Olympics in California.

Remotes

WGN Radio enjoys meeting its listeners. That means getting out of the studio, and not just to broadcast a baseball or football game, although that's part of it. For two hours before each Bears home game, we have a Pep Rally with live music, games, and prizes right outside the main gate at Soldier Field. Before away games, we broadcast our pep rallies from local restaurants. And a couple of times each baseball season, we do a pre-game few hours either under the stands or outside Wrigley Field.

We do remotes close to home and far afield. When the Chicago Theater reopened last fall, a major event in this city, WGN's Wally Phillips was there, live, for four hours. Lakefront festivities are fun, too. We broadcast more than seventy hours, over an eight-day period, from Taste of Chicago in Grant Park and twelve ours over two days from the Chicago Air and Water Show along a mile-long stretch of beach. Our nine remotes included three planes, two boats, and the tops of two tall buildings.

When there's an especially large crowd at an event, like the scores of thousands who come to these lakefront attractions, WGN offers even more service. The Trafficopter used in morning and afternoon drive to report weekday traffic is pressed into service for those specific events.

We spend a week each summer at the Illinois State Fair in Springfield, and we do remotes at thirty to forty county fairs in Illinois, Indiana, and Wisconisn each year. Among the other events where we do remotes are these:

• Chicago Auto Show: several shows over the week-long event.
• Schaumburg Water Carnival
• Rosemont Summer Fest
• Wheeling Family Fest (three days)
• Oak Brook All-American Bike Races
• Dupage County Bike-a-Thon

Call for Action

WGN Radio can make no unique claims about Call for Action. It began in New York many years ago and has spread across the country, volunteers helping people negotiate with the system, doing that work in cooperation with local broadcasters.

Westinghouse Broadcasting is an active supporter for Call for Action in several markets. It was active also in Chicago until it sold its AM property here. The new owners converted to a Spanish-language station. WGN Radio saw—and seized—the opportunity.

Call for Action (CFA) became part of the WGN Radio family officially in January 1986. During its eighteen months of operation with us, CFA has tallied 11,500 calls and has been able to resolve 3,100 listener problems. That success rate of 37 percent is impressive when the wide variety of complaints, many unfounded, is considered.

Support for CFA is expensive. Because it was not associated with WGN Radio when our new facilities were planned, we lease office space for the volunteers at prevailing Michigan Avenue rental rates. Other support—printing, postage, telephone—brings the total out-of-pocket cost to $20,000 annually. The value of the service CFA provides cannot be measured. If it could, this story would be even more impressive.

Community Involvement

There are a great many things WGN Radio people do off the air. Some of them may be mentioned and others not. Master-of-ceremonies duties are common. So are speeches. Farm Services Director Orion Samuelson makes sixty or so each year, all over the Midwest, giving members of his audience an opportunity to meet him face to face. He has been honored by more farm-related organizations than we can count. Recent awards for Bob Collins include the Richard J. Daley Award presented by the City of Chicago and the Citizen of the Year Award presented by the Pulitzer-Lerner Community Newspapers. Joseph Cardinal Bernardin selected Wally Phillips as winner of the Archbishop's Award for Outstanding Public Service.

And so it goes. WGN is what we hope and want a radio to be. It should be entertaining and informative, and we know it is both. Public interest means WGN has a stake in its community. And when we say, as we do on the air, "WGN Radio *is* Chicago," we mean it, and we say it with pride.

10

THE SMALL MARKET

It often takes much more ingenuity to make the concept of public interest work well in a small market. In this article, Lindsay Davis describes how this can be done in ways to make a broadcast station thrive. He works from the premise that a station's potential lies in "its ability to be that market"—and that is what public interest is all about. He specifically identifies programs that might assist the small-market broadcaster.

If there is anything to be learned from this piece, it is that the limitations that appear to confront the broadcaster in a small market are often self-imposed. By learning everything about the needs and aspirations of the small-market public, the broadcaster will discover those special services that only the station can offer. As the public-interest concept is carefully applied to a small market, it should lead to understanding the uniqueness of the public to be served. The successful broadcaster, therefore, will be able to reflect and interpret the local community in ways no other medium can. Under such circumstances, profit and public interest go hand in hand.

About the Author

Lindsay Wood Davis is General Manager of WSAD/WCUM in Middlebury, Vermont. He began his career in radio as a salesman at WGLB in Port Washington, Wisconsin, in 1967. After attending Northwestern University for four years, he became a salesman for KEED in Eugene, Oregon, in 1975, and moved on to become sales manager for KFMY in Eugene that same year.

In 1976 he joined his family-owned station, WSDR, in Sterling, Illinois, as vice president and general manager. He held that position until 1986, when he left to assume the general manager position at WSVA, Harrisonburg, Virginia.

Davis has been an active member of the broadcasting community and has served on the Board of Directors of the Illinois Broadcasters Association, Board of Advisors UPI, and the National Association of Broadcasters Legislative Liaison Committee.

He was a winner of United Press International's Best Illinois Editorial Award for 1983 and of the Illinois Broadcasters Association's Silver Dome Award for Best Radio Editorial in 1984.

He has spoken and participated in many broadcast seminars including those sponsored by the National Association of Broadcasters, 1982; NAB/Radio Programming Conference, 1980, 1984; NRBA/NAB/RPC, 1984; Michigan Association of Broadcasters, 1986; and Southern Illinois and Northern Illinois Universities, 1982, 1983, and 1984.

Public Interest: Understanding the Small Market

LINDSAY WOOD DAVIS

When a picture is painted by a brush, it's really produced by the individual bristles that make up that brush. Good small-market radio is like that. A whole lot of little bristles make up the brush that will allow you to paint the picture—hopefully in black, not red.

A local small-market station has a lot of markets to serve. In fact, a small-market station really has a much greater responsibility to serve than its large-market brethren. A large market has enough stations so that each can target a specific segment and remain, or become, profitable, while meeting its federal mandate to serve "the public." In a small market, with so many fewer signals but almost as many available target audiences, or "publics," the small-market station must serve many more masters in order to meet its obligation. I'm suggesting that you have to choose specific markets—a whole series of them—and fully serve them. I am *not* suggesting you be full-service radio, though if you do this really well, that's what you'll be reinventing. Rather I'm suggesting you fully serve a series of individual audiences and sell the resulting programs, at premium rates, to the clients that will be so very obvious. For instance, the classic noontime farm shows commanded amazing rates because the clients knew it was the right buy without deep research to tell them so. What about cooking shows, auto repair shows, computer shows, VCR reports, author's corners, wine shows, restaurant reviews, skin-diving reports, industrial and economic development updates, gardening tips, travel reports, solar power news, fashion updates, hunting and fishing reports, wood-heat tips, auto-racing shows, horse-racing shows, dog-racing shows, bowling reports, animal-care tips, movie reviews, boating reports, ag weather, flying weather, highway weather, sailing weather, investment programs, insurance programs, health-care programs, local history, and a lot more, many specific to your area? Here I'll surprise you! Every one of the programs I listed—*every one*—is a program that I have aired on one of my stations, and in every case sold at a premium rate on a long-term contract—*every one*!

What I have just described to you is narrowcasting—though nobody ever thought of it as that—and, coupled with the traditional news-weather-sports-entertainment mix, gives you a traditional full-service format. Again, I'm not in any way advocating a full-service format, but I'm saying that broadcasters of all market sizes should fully serve the audience you have. In a small market—Sterling, Illinois; Harri-sonburg, Virginia; Middlebury, Vermont; and places far smaller—we don't really choose our audiences. We dance with who brung us—'cause there's no other choice. We in small markets have always been narrowcasters in the purest sense. It's just that we've served so many narrow interests, so many small wedges of the pie, that we've made a whole pie out of it.

There are those who probably look upon my ideas as old-fashioned radio, hopelessly out of date. Where, for instance, is any talk of the twin gods of ratings-based programming technique—quarter-hour maintenance and cume building? Well, though I agree that these techniques do look to increase cume rather than share, I challenge you to get a big share without the cume to drive the quarter-hour engine. In small markets, this whole argument is usually a waste of breath because the real make of a small market station's *potential* is its ability to *be that market*.

A true story (I was there) about the best Halloween party costume I ever saw. It took place at the Springfield, Oregon, American Legion Hall at the Annual Freakers' Ball, held for years by Ken Kesey and the Merry Pranksters. I arrived at the party and soon saw a physically beautiful woman dressed completely in a black leotard, complete with a tight-fitting hood; she had a strong presence. The whole room seemed to act in concert with her actions. Her most obvious trait was that hanging in front of her face—completely hiding her face, in fact—was a mirror. When I finally approached her and asked her what she was supposed to represent, I saw my face in that mirror. And she answered by saying, "I'm you."

Good small-market radio is a lot like that woman—whose mirror turned out to be one-way glass—a two-way mirror. She was a reflection of those in the room; yet, her presence was designed to be so total that the actions reflected became as much *caused* by her as *reflected* by her. And while she reflected those around her, she was able to maintain a clear vision as to where she was and where she was going.

That's right: reflect the community, but in bite-size pieces like a mirror ball. You'll dazzle 'em!

When you do all this reflecting and targeting and involving, you're going to bring a new partner to the party—your clients. Because in this type of programming rather than a formatted radio station, aiming at narrow interests within the confines of the broader community, your sponsors' advertisements (Can we please get rid of the word "spots" completely from our vocabulary?) become not an intrusion, but an integral part of the program. Let's remember that in the effort to serve that audience fully your definition of news and information really has to expand to information that affects your listeners' daily lives. This is most obvious on the local small-market level, but isn't that what news is anyway?

I firmly believe in an aggressive, well-staffed news department, but I've found that at most radio stations, the news department is bad news. Face it folks, the news department at the normal radio station is bad news—expensive, unnecessary, downright counterproductive, at least in the minds of the 1980s deregulated broadcaster.

When news is off in its own orbit, news can be all those things. But when news becomes one with programming, sales, and community involvement—part of a single process—it becomes part of a tremendously powerful entity—good radio. Has it ever occurred to you that a unique sale at a local car dealership, a special or unusual deal at the furniture store, or a truly new service at the local bank *is* news, news in its purest form? News is information that affects your listeners' lives . . . the more so if it affects their daily lives. You must be ready to serve your listeners fully with your radio station, not just the news department, or advertising, or programming, but the whole station. You must work together.

It's this area that almost always gets me the most arguments, especially from news people, as you might guess, though never my own. There's always wild protesting, frothing at the mouth, that I'm prostituting the concept of news; that while I'd have *my* reporters kowtowing to the wishes of our clients, the pure news, the real news if you will, will go uncovered. Well, horse manure! Let's realize that this kind of "news you can use" aspect of reporting can only be done in the context of a strong, independent news department—no exceptions. Aggressively reporting the stories that people have to know about even though they may not want to know. My news staffs have won as many awards for spot news, in-depth series, and documentaries as most small-market stations in the nation and won both state and national awards for hard-hitting editorials on such "soft" subjects as the need to arrest a local police chief and being the first to advocate the forced merging of a public hospital in one town with a private one in another. People have to notice you, and a strong commitment to involvement in your community, to its very fabric, can make your every act noticed.

The strong local news department involved with all aspects of the radio station, and therefore the community, can provide that community with a voice for not just its "defeats" (failings and foibles which must be covered), but also and maybe more important, for its "victories"—its solutions, its bright spots, giving the town a way to say to itself "We're O.K.!"

It's the interworking of all the aspects of a local radio station that can make a discussion of its future success almost absurd. Unless the community dies, the station just about can't. The term I'm driving for here is "synergy," and its converse is departmental division. A synergystic broadcaster is going to fight constantly against the "fortified village" clannishness so prevalent in many facilities. How can you act in concert if nobody knows what anybody else is doing? You synergistically work together in your station and in and with your community.

The kind of targeted sales that result from this kind of programming will and do allow an average unit rate of amazing levels. In Illinois, in a rural town of 16,000 on a 500-watt station, we now average over $25.00 per unit, and in Virginia that average unit rose almost 150 percent in just sixteen months. Your total unit count will probably decline, but the average unit rate increase will more than offset that reduction.

Let's understand, however, that my kind of programming is (1) people intensive, and (2) time-consuming to establish. Don't for one minute think that you can raise the "concerned broadcaster's" flag and expect everything to be fine in six or twelve months. If that's your goal, I'd recommend you get out of radio and try investment banking.

Maybe we will go the way of the buckboard, paddlewheeler, steam engine, dirigible, and all those other "basics" of America. After all, death is just nature's way of saying "Howdy." Maybe a better way has been found, maybe we are an anachronism, but how can a medium that allows us to communicate affordably and inform the mass of America be an anachronism in this age of communications and information? It's this concept of information and communication that most intrigues me, especially among and between the small businesses that make a small market go.

Of all the world's major industrial centers—Europe, Japan, Brazil and the United States—only in America are new, absolutely new, jobs being created. In the other industrial centers what few jobs are created are simply replacements of previous positions in other fields.

Government regulations of the production environment in the other industrial societies has ordained this as the continuing truth of non-competition, proving again and again the economic dictum that those who have the most to gain from regulation are the regulated. Yet business America continues to produce new jobs, not just replacement jobs, but real net increases. These new positions continue to be spewed forth from that fantastic engine that surrounds us—that *is* us—small-business America. The future of successful profitable local radio rests right there. We are how small business talks to America, we are how small business can best communicate its hopes and dreams, because we are small business. Good radio—great radio AM or FM, large market or small market—understands its role as inter-locuter in this big community minstrel show that we put on every day, sign on to sign off.

In the very early days of the late NRBA, their counsel, Thomas Schattenfield of Arent, Fox and Kinzer, would discuss broadcasters faced with today's new reality. Schattenfield told the story of the Wizard of Oz. Dorothy grew up in Kansas where everything was in black and white. Then she was whisked away to Oz , where everything was in color and the possibilities endless. All Dorothy really wanted, though, was to return to the old days of Kansas, the old predictable days of black and white. Well, for us in radio, the old days of black and white are really the old days of black or red. The new choice is a new world of Oz, where everything is in color and the possibilities endless, or the old days of Kansas where everything was so black and blue.

Give me Oz every time because life's more fun when you can paint your picture in the black using all the colors of opportunity. It's life or death, and I'll choose life. Living is in the public interest!

11

SMALL MARKET
BROADCASTING

Considering the more than 10,000 radio stations in the United States, it is not difficult to imagine that public interest comes to be defined as programming that interests the public. So writes Charles E. Wright in his description of what public interest means for the small market. In this article, he begins with the big picture: federal legislation and FCC regulation. He quickly narrows his description, however, to encompass what public interest really means in the small market.

Since small-market stations cannot afford professional research, he points out that listener mail, as well as surveys at guest speaker luncheons and community colleges can help. He expresses concern that programmers sometimes listen to other programmers in setting up their station's formats rather than pay attention to the interests of the local public. For example, he notes that in most small markets obituaries are one of the most popular programs, as are births and the scores of the local basketball teams. Local news plays an important role. And, as he points out, public interest means that the station becomes "the catalyst for all good things"—community spirit, conscience, party line, and so forth.

As much as any other institution, the small-market broadcaster plays a role in the local community. The station becomes a mouthpiece, a source of information in normal times and emergencies, a local resource that need not be overwhelmed by distant voices. For the broadcaster, as for any other retailer in a small community, good business practice means being important to the local community.

About the Author

Charles E. Wright is president and general manager of WBYS, Canton, Illinois. He began his broadcasting career in 1941 as an announcer/writer at KTVC in Tuscon, Arizona. After spending three years in the U.S. Navy during World War II, he received a B.A. degree in history and political science from the University of Puget Sound in Tacoma, Washington.

His extensive experience in radio has included broadcast journalism, engineering, programming, management, and sales. He arrived at Canton in 1954 and has managed WBYS for thirty-three of its forty years of operation. During that time he has written and aired a daily five-minute commentary seven days a week. Since 1960 WBYS has received over forty-five awards from Associated Press for news and public affairs programming.

His industry activities have been the Illinois Broadcasters Association, including IBA president (1979) and director emeritus (awarded in 1980)—the only member with that status; National Association of Broadcasters, radio director for Illinois and Wisconsin (1977–1981); Illinois Associated Press Association president (1978–1979); Associated Press Broadcasters Association (National) Board Member.

His community activities include United Way Board of Directors; Canton Park District Board of Commissioners; Canton Planning and Zoning Commission and other city committees; YWCA Public Relations Committee, and First Congregational Church Council. In March 1982, Charles Wright received the Citizen of the Year award from the Canton Area Chamber of Commerce.

Public Interest Broadcasting in the Small Market

CHARLES E. WRIGHT

There are dozens of formats used by the more than 10,000 radio stations in the United States. Each station seeks its own audience with its programming. If people listen to a station to any degree, there is a public-interest factor in the broad sense. Defining the public interest may be as difficult as defining pornography. Put simply, it's programming that interests the public and is of service to the public.

The public interest was a bedrock requirement for the issuing of a radio station license from the very beginning. It is a paramount philosophy of the Communications Act of 1934. One need only refer to the annual volumes of the *Federal Communications Reports* that cite decisions where a contest was involved and invariably the grounds for granting a license to the successful applicant includes the broadcasting in the "public interest, convenience and necessity."

For many years the FCC required radio stations to classify programming into a minimum of seven categories. They were Entertainment, Religion, Agricultural, Educational, News, Discussion, and Talks. A big distinction was made between sustaining (noncommercial) and commercial programs. Further reporting had to be done in the following categories: Network Commercial, Network Sustaining, Recorded Commercial, Recorded Sustaining, Wire Commercial, Wire Sustaining, Live Commercial, and Live Sustaining. It was a real ordeal to keep program logs for two years with such information for a composite week to be analyzed at license renewal time.

In March 1946 the FCC published a celebrated document known as *Public Service Responsibility of Broadcasters*, more commonly known as the Blue Book. It was the result of a study directed by Dr.

Charles Siepmann, formerly of the British Broadcasting Corporation. The Commission was seeking a basis for the evaluation of radio program service.

An interesting story used to be told by the late Ed Jacker, who operated a 250-watt station in Chicago that broadcast ethnic programming. On his license renewal he did not show any agricultural programming. He contended to the Commission that his station could not be heard beyond the city limits of Chicago, and the only agriculture his listeners were concerned with was the growing of flowers in their window boxes.

In time the Blue Book faded away and the logging requirements went the way of "The following announcement is electrically transcribed." Essentially, the Commission turned the programming of stations over to the licensee, as it found it could not prescribe the standards of public interest programming because that would take away from the creativity and flexibility of the American system of broadcasting.

The programming that the broadcaster developed to serve the market replaced that which had been imposed by government edict. Former Chairman Mark Fowler believed strongly in the marketplace forces that give the broadcaster the opportunity to fulfill the mandate of the license to operate in the "public interest, convenience and necessity."

Public-interest programming in the small market is different from that in larger markets. It is more "down home," more neighborly, and gets into the nooks and crannies of the community. Large-market stations can't afford to devote the time to the type of programs that are the real "dial setters" for a small-market station. Many broadcasters make the mistake of not going into their communities and learning what the people are interested in hearing on the station.

In 1981 the Associated Press published its *Radio Listening Attitudes* for its members. It was compiled by Brad Kalbfeld of the AP, and one section dealt with *Interest in Activities Information*. Forty-six subjects were rated on whether the respondents were very interested. When a station learns the interests and programs to satisfy those interests, it will have a much larger and more responsive audience.

Most small-market stations can't afford a research firm to conduct a survey, but valuable information may be obtained at very small cost. A survey of listeners' interests can be made by mail. Along with their interests, valuable demographic data can be obtained by giving a prize to one of the respondents. When someone from the station speaks at a local club, take survey forms along to pass out, and collect them before leaving. On a station's call-in show listeners can respond to what they want to hear about on the station. Community colleges are a good source for research on listening interests. A station must know what turns the listeners on, so that they will turn the station on.

Programmers sometimes program for other programmers. Nowhere is that more evident than at a programmers' convention. Just listen to them talk about their formats. Programmers should program to listeners, and what the listener wants may not be what some other programmer thinks should be programmed. Programmers in large markets might consider a small market's strongest programming as "pretty hokey," but if you're running a shoe store and the women want purple shoes, even if you hate purple, you had better stock purple shoes if you want to sell.

In most small markets one of the most popular programs is obituaries. The listeners want to know who died, who the survivors are, when the visitation is, when and where the funeral will be, where the burial will be, and to which memorial they may contribute. In many communities radio is the only way listeners can learn the details because the time of the death is out of sync with the publication dates of the local newspaper.

In many of the little communities near the small-market station the birth of a child, the death of a citizen, or the score of a basketball game are the biggest news events of the week. Broadcasting that information is serving the public interest.

Public-interest programming comes in all lengths, sizes, and shapes, and can be just a few seconds of vital information pertaining to a broken water main to an actuality with someone in authority explaining the meaning of something that is significant. It can be part of a newscast or something the disc jockey talks about between records. Public-interest information between records can hold the listener who otherwise would tune in for news only.

The kind of music format a station has will determine in part what kinds of public-interest information should be broadcast. Listeners to a rock station have different interests from those who listen to a beautiful music station.

When a station and its personnel become involved in the community, the public-interest opportunities will flow into the station. Public-interest programming becomes full-service programming. It's news about what went on at the city council meeting or school board meeting. It's about the Sunday school teacher who is retiring, the cutting down of a tree that dates back to the turn of the century, or the wrecking of an old building to make room for a new parking lot or whatever. When was it built? Who built it? What was it used for? Interesting! Public-interest information is about school closing in the winter, a lost dog everyone knows, finding answers for people, telling people how to write to their congressman. The broadcasting of school menus and those at the nutrition centers for senior citizens serve the public interest. A station is on the right wavelength with the public when it tells about the good turn someone does for a stranger, promotes a benefit for an organ transplant, puts the United Way over the top, helps pass a referendum to build a new school, or promotes helping a farmer who's in the hospital to get his crops in.

The public interest is served when the station becomes the catalyst for good things. The station becomes the generator of the community spirit. It's the pulse of the community; its conscience, pulpit, forum, party line—and it breathes life into every community activity.

At the Illinois Broadcasters Association convention in Chicago in October 1987, the editor-in-chief of *Channels Magazine*, Les Brown, spoke in part about why people tune in to radio and TV stations. He asked that since people now own so many records and video cassettes, why do they listen to radio and TV? His answer was the people want to be "plugged into the outside world." Public-interest information and features are the outside world for listeners.

In order for a station to broadcast public interest information and features effectively, it must have a qualified staff. Much of the information in the public-interest category must come from a qualified news staff. If a station does not have an experienced news reporter and is depending on an announcer or disc jockey whose world does not extend beyond the music charts, the station will be in a compromised position when it comes to significant events such as tornadoes, hurricanes, earthquakes, and accidents involving toxic materials. Continuous information must be provided in such events to serve the public interest. The station should have a qualified staff member who has the time to get the necessary information and be able to relate it to the local listener. That person should be adept at taking huge national figures on budgets and debts and converting them to a per person basis and for the home country. A multi-million-dollar figure doesn't mean a lot to the average person until we say that it represents $25,000 for every man, woman, and child in the nation.

It's important for a station to have every printed pamphlet or book on local history and have contacts with people with this kind of knowledge. Events and information can then be tied to the roots of the people and the community, a hot button in most small towns.

For much too long some in broadcasting have thought of public-interest programming as dull, uninteresting, and a listener tune-out. This may be a carry-over from the early-day pontifical public affairs programs that ran a half hour or more, opened with pompous music and an announcer in sonorous tones sounding as if he were Moses proclaiming the Ten Commandments from atop Mount Sinai. Good public-interest programming will be the talk of the town, and the station will be the focus of attention. It's good for the community and good for a station.

The good public-interest broadcaster knows how the community is put together, and when someone is pinched, he will know who the people are who will say "ouch." He will have the guts to editorialize on local issues and will be fair to those with differing viewpoints.

A good public interest broadcaster is a vital force in the community, playing an exciting, beneficial role with no worry about how many distant signals come into the market because the broadcaster is serving the people.

12

PUBLIC INTEREST
MEANS MANY
THINGS

Chuck Harrison, now retired from a long career in broadcasting, observes in these personal reflections that while the concept of public interest can be interpreted in many ways, there are common elements in its implementation that include station personnel, careful planning, and community involvement before success can be assured. To support this approach he offers three examples of successful projects in medium markets.

Again, the reader will find some enterprising projects described in detail that illustrate how a station can relate to the community in a cooperative spirit. In one instance, the objective of the project was not to raise money but to save lives. Harrison offers specific examples where community members have become actual participants, if not the major players in station projects.

As with large and small markets, the medium-market station can find ways of interpreting the public-interest obligation to assure prominence in the community marketplace. The active role that the concept of public interest plays in the business of broadcasting is good for business.

About the Author

Charles F. "Chuck" Harrison graduated from high school in Rock Island, Illinois, in 1937. While in high school, he was active in speech, debate, and dramtics. During this period he worked part time, mostly in the summer, at WHBF.

He attended Augustana College before leaving to accept a position at a radio station in Poynette, Wisconsin. After two years, he returned to WHBF as an announcer and stayed there for twelve years with time out for service in the U.S. Air Force in 1942–1945 as a pilot instructor. In 1946 Harrison created the first News Department for WHBF.

In 1952 he went to WING, Dayton, then on to radio and television positions in Philadelphia, where he stayed for five years until he moved to Miami. He moved to Peoria when WMBD–TV was established, as in his previous assignments, became the news director and anchor. When the station was sold, he remained in Peoria, moving to WEEK–TV where he stayed for eleven years as news director and anchor.

In 1969 Harrison went to WAVE Radio and Television in Louisville, Kentucky. In 1971 he accepted a position with WGN, Chicago. He became president of RTNDA in 1972–1973. He joined WIFR-TV in Rockford, Illinois, in 1973 as broadcast manager and vice president. He then returned to the station (now WHBF-TV) where he had started as a high school student, becoming vice president and general manager until his retirement in 1987.

Programming in the Public Interest Means Many Things

CHARLES F. "CHUCK" HARRISON

Any discussion of the activities arising from the broadcaster's "public-interest" obligation can follow a number of different paths. Does it mean "Public Affairs," "Public Service," "Community Service," or another of a dozen titles given this type of programming? For our purposes, let us agree that names don't mean much; it is the content we are concerned about. Feel free to apply the title that best fits your background, your station. Why not? I'm about to confine the subject to a rather narrow field.

Public Affairs usually includes public service announcements. We aren't going to spend any time discussing the two-second ID or thirty-second spots. There is nothing wrong with them. A few stations delight in logging those slides with a tiny bit of audio recognizing the existence of a charitable or service agency; it may be all they do.

Similarly, there is that special type of program, the "Public Affairs Interview." It may be part of a noon news block, or carried as a filler when weekend football runs over. Often, it is aired just before the national anthem at sign-off. While audiences may be very small, the information may be of high quality if the interviewer is interested as well as competent.

Despite the placement of these programs in slots where the availability of viewers is small, they can have great impact. One station in Texas decided to put such programming after its 10 o'clock news on Sunday night. The manager was the host. Viewers were invited to criticize the programming of the station, and the boss was there to dodge the bullets! He didn't dodge the tough questions and comments. On occasion, he even apologized for an action the viewers did not like. When answers were not available, he found them and made sure they were presented the next week. It didn't take long for this Public Affairs program to be one of the highest rated on that station. More important, it remained a successful offering for years.

So far, I seem to have eliminated public service spots and programs as topics for discussion. What is left? For this purpose we will be talking about a higher order of Public Affairs, using markets of varying size to illustrate and approach to Public Affairs, a cooperation of elements within the station, and planning that produces unusual results.

Public Affairs—An Exciting Show "Under the Big Top"

When a public affairs activity helps to create the image of the entire station, it has gone far above the average. When that same effort is highly entertaining, collects millions for community betterment, and nearly a hundred agencies compete for grants to further their work, that station has done something unique.

WHAS-TV, Louisville, started its Crusade for Children about thirty-four years ago. Each year it grew. Each year new elements were added. I saw the Crusade almost twenty years ago. The fundamentals have not changed. It is a weekend, twenty-six hour event, preceded by fifty-two weeks of preparation. Every member of the staff supports the effort in some way. Once the crusade is over, the station goes on the air with a full accounting of all monies collected, expenses paid, and grants made. The same information is presented in the Sunday editions of Kentucky's largest newspaper. Last year, the income was nearly $2.5 million. Expenses were under 5 percent. The proceeds of this activity are allocated by five clergymen who, themselves, are recognized as community leaders. So far, some $29 million have gone to grants for children suffering for every kind of affliction.

This Public Affairs activity has married the station to the people in forty-four counties in Indiana and Kentucky. Two hundred fire departments in those counties are a vital part of the effort. Who can measure the loyalty to the station the other fifty-one weeks of the year? Because of its history of success for so many years, those who watched when younger are now leaving bequests "for the children." These bequests now amount to more than $1 million dollars. Yes, there is a special plaque in the station's lobby with the name of each donor.

It is the most successful single-station telethon in America. It deserves to be. One man, Vic Sholis, started it. As general manager, he convinced the owners they should eliminate all commercial income and donate the time and effort of the telethon to begin the Crusade.

Impact

The telethon itself touched every community in the broadcast area. Impact? Little Bonnieville, Kentucky, has only 300 residents. Its first department brought in $4,000. That is $13 for every man, woman, and child in the village! The departments vie for trophies given to those who show the greatest increase over last year. They are displayed with deserved pride.

Service clubs in the region make special efforts to be part of the Crusade. The Red Men's Lodge in New Albany gave more than $35,000, and members made bequests of $201,000. General Electric workers gave $80,000. The Catholic Archdiocese contributed $97,500.

These examples illustrate the depth of the impact on various elements in the communities. There is, however, no way to measure the impact that the work of the station has had in individual homes. Add for yourself the home with children directly benefiting from the funds collected; throw in $2 million to state universities for the training of teachers of handicapped students; other millions for life-saving equipment given to the University of Kentucky School of Medicine and Kosair Children's Hospital.

Effort

When Vic Sholis came up with his idea, the effort seemed almost too much to handle. Remember, TV staffs were small back then. The Crusade grew because outside groups, all volunteers, helped share the load. From the beginning, this effort was pegged on making it a community effort, not just a station activity. It began as a studio production, something the station could handle. While this year's production included two remote stages as well as the studio, this did not happen overnight.

Community Involvement

WHAS-TV did what it set out to do. First, it gave. Gave up revenue, donated its time and facilities, offered its talent and complete staff. And for what? Its goal was to show a need to all its viewers, show a way to meet that need, and *involve* large numbers of individuals and organizations in that work.

There are forty-four counties in the station's service area. In reaching out to every segment of its "community," WHAS-TV has created an empathic response, amplified over thirty-four years. That is truly unique.

Another Example

What of the station that does yeoman service of various kinds, all year long? Frankly, the list is long, very long. Why do I pick WSAZ-TV to be the example? It is one of the Lee Enterprises, Inc., stations. Lee is active in both print and broadcasting. Investors are happy with the solid, steady growth of the company. Competitors have reason to be less joyous. This station has had a long and lustrous image as a quality operation. Bos Johnson built a reputation around the country for his news operation there. When he left to become a professor of journalism, Bob Brunner moved up from within, and their quality of news service didn't miss a beat. Finally, the fairly new manager there, Gary Schmedding, is from Illinois. He is a respected member of the broadcast fraternity. When ownership, employees and management are of such high calibre, nice things happen. It is also most true when bad events occur.

They did. Unemployment hit their market. The jobless rate hit a modern-day high. WSAZ pulled the plug on 4 1/2 hours of prime-time programming for a Job-A-Thon. It was a total-station effort with over 1,000 people in their service area—West Virginia, Kentucky and Ohio—taking part. Three hundred people went on camera to describe themselves and the positions they were seeking.

All telethons come to an end as this one did, but the needs remain. The station continues the work it started. Every weekday it airs "Job Bank" with the posting of openings on both early and late news. So far, it has announced more than 3,000 job openings in its service area.

Because activity of this type in public affairs can alter the course of a station, note that this has occurred in *every* example discussed here. The synergism created in one special effort creates a new and larger goal. The larger waves of success call for repetition.

WSAZ excels in efforts directed toward education. It is a Business Partner in Education and sponsors a "Just Say No" club at a local school. Its biggest moment comes in May as it honors the top graduates in the viewing area with its "Best of the Class" project. In 1987 it hosted a luncheon honoring almost 200 students and produced forty-eight different public service announcements saluting their academic achievements. The project began with the co-sponsorship of General Motors. Budget cutbacks at GM forced the automaker to withdraw, so WSAZ picked up the project at its own expense. Now they have added a current events quiz, "News Game." Every week the station mails the game with thirty-two current events questions to 500 teachers in the coverage area.

Without going into detail, here are some additional areas where WSAZ serves its ADI (Area of Dominant Influence) on a regular basis.

The News Department has aired a weekly feature, attracting many Big Brothers and Big Sisters with profiles of different children. New Director Bob Brunner also reports on "special needs" adoption cases. A holiday-season anti—drunk driving campaign brought a Presidential Citation for Private Sector Initiative and a first-place award from the station's peers in Ad Club competition.

Sometimes projects have to be revamped. A Holiday Food Drive didn't work out well the first time. This year the plan was scrapped and reworked to meet the needs of a large geographical area better. This time convenience stores will be used as collection points. Each store manager will turn the food over to a local collection agency.

WSAZ has also been involved in one activity that is quite rare— participating in a combined effort involving a large group of broadcasters. When a flood nearly wiped out the northern part of West Virginia two years ago, *every television station*, including the public stations, joined together for a major telethon to benefit flood victims. Show me a list of times when fourteen television and forty radio stations have banded together in common cause. They had a goal of $1 million. They went over that goal by $700,000.

In summary, here is a fine station in a medium-sized market. It doesn't have many of the blessings of an operation in the Sun Belt. It has more than its share of the problems that belabor the country's midsection. It has energetically done something where its signal could make a difference. Yes, it made a whole raft of public service announcements, but they were just the first step or a pleasant add-on to their plan. Yes, it jumped in when unemployment reached the crisis stage, but it didn't "jump in and jump out." The work goes on. When a food drive came up short of its hopes, it assessed the project, made changes to assure a wider scope and greater success.

Last But Not Least

In admitting to fifty years in broadcasting, I always want to go back and correct the typo. It can't be. But it is. During that time, a few "golden call letters" have consistently stood high in radio and television. KDKA, WTVJ, WGN, WBAP, WFAA are only a few. Feel free to add your favorite. I am adding one more because I like to think I hate them!

When I was a young man working in Philadelphia, I was asked to audition for an opening at WCCO, Minneapolis. Now those are golden call letters! Sure, I went. Yes, I wanted that job. I didn't get it. They told me that I looked too much and sounded too much like "Chick" on their staff. And I go by "Chuck." It may be that they were just finding a nice way to let me down. Though losing hurt, I had to accept the fact that they don't make mistakes.

In the thirty-five years since then, I have had increasing respect for that station and admit I only hated losing the chance to be part of a dynamic, successful, and caring broadcast combination in a major market. It evened out later when I joined WGN radio and TV.

If one is looking for a market where competition makes it beautiful for the viewer, look no further. There is no doubt that one can find great public affairs products aired by every television station. There is no intent to denigrate the others; it is just that WCCO has done so much, so well, and for so long, I could not look elsewhere when looking for the keystone of this piece.

Project Lifesaver is just a name for a public affairs venture. It began simply enough. Too many die on Minnesota highways. What can the station do?

Here is what that venture accomplished. American Automobile Association (AAA) did a survey and found that 83 percent of the respondents were aware of Project Lifesaver. How many successful ad campaigns can claim this kind of success?

Unlike the routine public affairs project, this one had complete cooperation of the state police, unique cooperation coming from the *St. Paul Pioneer Press and Dispatch* and newspapers across the state. A major ad agency caught the fever early and donated its expertise. Add the encouragement of forty state organizations and this pot begins to boil.

The project began with a major documentary looking at 610 highway deaths in 1985. It focused on the stories told by victims and their families of the pain and suffering caused by highway accidents, most of which involved a driver under the influence of alcohol. "Sudden Death" and other specials followed, aired by WDSE in Duluth, KCMT in Alexandria, and KAWE-TV in Bemidji as these stations joined the project.

Worthy as the project was in itself, this was just the "kick-off." Shortly after, a memorial service at the State Capitol called for action to reduce the senseless deaths on Minnesota highways. Planners had four goals. The first week they wanted to convince motorists they were mortal and vulnerable to the dangers in driving. The next week featured a call to persuade everyone to begin the seat-belt habit. Week three was devoted to teaching citizens how to prevent drunk driving. The final week was aimed at preventing motor-vehicle crashes anywhere in Minnesota during the Memorial Day Weekend.

Every day during this campaign, layers of activity were directed toward a target—every individual in the state. Thirteen reporters from the St. Paul newspaper worked on their "crusade." That means major articles in every edition, interviews with survivors of accidents, opinion pieces and columns on traffic-safety issues, and full-page house ads promoting Project Lifesaver.

WCCO television followed its documentary with special reports on its newscasts and seven (count them), seven specials. Three were aired specifically for students; the other aired in prime evening hours. WCCO radio also played a major role in the project, using special guests and news specials throughout the four weeks.

Are you beginning to catch the flavor of this effort? Here you have newspapers and radio and television stations across a state working on a project of major proportions. Statistics are usually boring until they concern your wallet or your bottom line. What stations will dedicate 9,000 hours of work time on one public affairs project at an estimated cost of $150,000? How often will that same station toss in about $450,000 worth of broadcast time for PSAs in one project? Is it routine for that same station to spend another $40,000 for out-of-pocket costs?

As Project Lifesaver grew, others joined. Ruhr/Paragon Inc. gave the entire resources of its agency to develop a strategy for reaching the public. In making the public service anouncements and other materials, Robert L. Jones, president, said, "Our goal isn't just to provide reminders, but to develop a new strategy that will change behavior, encourage intervention, apply peer pressure to those who do not exercise care [when driving]."

The St. Paul Companies wrote checks for the production of posters, pledge cards, seat belt reminder stickers, and brochures. All this material was made available to schools, employer groups, churches, hospitals, and other groups interested in being part of the program.

It all began with a simple conversation between John Finnegan, editor of the St. Paul newspaper, Roon Handberg, VP of WCCO–TV, and Clayt Kaufman, Senior VP of WCCO radio. Planning began months before it became a public activity. The effort became state-wide. Impact? The goals Jones voiced were reached, and they were tough goals. Changing behavior is much different from exposing a problem or discussing a community need. But they succeeded. It was obvious that once the "Prjoect Lifesaver" concept was born, it had to be broken into smaller digestible segments. Each participant knew the general topic (seat belt, drunk driving, or whatever), and the individual "teams" worked in their area of expertise. I still wonder which team ordered, cut, packaged, and delivered hundreds of thousands of yellow ribbons to thousands of businesses, restaurants, grocery stores, banks, and pizza parlors. Imagine all those cars with yellow ribbons on the antennas!

Broadcasters knew as well about the bumper stickers. One Boy

Scout Troop ordered 2,000 seat-belt bumper stickers to hand out at a car wash.

All this demonstrates that WCCO television and its friends get an "A" in the final category I have arbitrarily used as a guide—community involvement. The stations, the newspaper, and all the other major participants decided that the state of Minnesota was *their* community. They didn't use voice, picture, and print to talk *to* their constituents. They went to the people with ribbons, brochures, and arguments in hand. They can be proud of the way the people responded.

People still die on the highway in Minnesota, and drunk driving remains an unsolved problem. There is now way to assess the number of lives saved by Project Lifesaver, but one small test indicates the validity of the campaign. Only 18 percent of the people wore seat belts according to the state survey. Some wag got the idea of a contest between the cities of Minneapolis and St. Paul over the wearing of seat belts. At the end of two weeks *three* times as many drivers of the Twin Cities were complying as before.

Summary and Some Conclusions

We have seen three examples of public service of the highest order. You can certainly add stations and projects from your own area and knowledge. This discussion carefully avoided any station from my state. How can I pick from good stations and friends in Chicago, Champaign, or Peoria while ignoring their friendly competitors? At my age, I can't risk losing any more friends! The public service examples used were my choice because they varied widely in market size, geography, and types of programs and campaigns.

They had common ground, however. Each had a long history of our subject matter. Each holds a consistent record of public service. The public they serve became an integral part of the work. We can't look at any of these stations and say it was an annual Crusade for Children, a documentary called "Sudden Death," or a Campaign on Unemployment that made that station recognized at home or elsewhere as a special broadcaster. Year after year, each one has "done its job" and improved in technique and product.

You have noted that no problem or need was approached from a feeling that a minimal effort would be the contribution. Recall an earlier comment about "total station," combined effort. I feel compelled to comment on the internal impact on staff. As television has grown, departments have grown, and some now have brick walls to separate them from others. Part of this is normal —salesmen really don't have great interest in engineering. Since news is busy and preoccupied, the problems of programming or costs of operation don't come readily to mind. It is, however, a great change from the early days, and some of it is not healthy. When most of the separate entities within a station are intimately involved in an important, prestigious undertaking, everyone benefits. Perhaps this is part of the reason for picking the stations used in this article. Initially they used "whole staff" projects. The only brick walls now are on the outside of the building. A Robert Frost poem has a line like this: "Something there is about a wall that wants it down."

True, but once built, they don't come down easily. A project involving large numbers of staff may encourage them to look over the wall at what's going on elsewhere in the station.

There is a different kind of brick wall in public service broadcasting that needs to be addressed. Public service has long been sacrosanct. No commercials, no sponsorship! In the future, why not?

The mass audience of free broadcasting is now a little smaller percentage of total viewing. The competitive forces will grow. The cost of inventive, important public service will increase. There are today few barter series being offered the industry. Good grief, they contain commercials! We know there isn't any free lunch, and stations wishing to do more—and better—public service programming may well want to rethink their positions. True Value Hardware has already done its thinking and become rather active in this field. In the decade ahead, doors will open wider for sponsorship of important public service programming planned far enough in advance to satisfy needs of station representatives and agencies.

All that is left for me is to supply quickly the methods for copying success in some other market. It may be great flattery, but it's the quickest way to failure. What works in Louisville isn't the answer in Des Moines. Minneapolis isn't St. Louis.

If you look at group operation, print or broadcast, the best ones have a policy of *local* determination of what goes in the news hole or broadcast schedule. That is how it must be.

13

THE INSIDE OF
PUBLIC INTEREST

In this somewhat light-hearted and personal essay, Jim Oetken writes with the perspective of a medium-market television station. He begins by observing that most who work in broadcasting are more committed than the average to a public-service orientation. He links this commitment with the general desire most have to work for a "winning" organization. That does not necessarily mean the most profitable station, although good public service in terms of strong local news and number one ratings can lead to high profits.

The drift of his observations, however, is that the station's staff should be the starting point for any program or project created in the public interest. Successful community projects require that all the station's staff be enthusiastic, sharing the vision and receiving recognition. And whatever else is said, idealism plays a part in the process.

About the Author

Jim Oetken is a native of Louisville, Kentucky. He was graduated from Bellarmine College and attended Creighton University for graduate studies in psychology.

Oetken began his broadcast career in 1961 at WAVE Radio in Louisville. In 1966 he was transferred to sister station WFRV-TV in Green Bay, Wisconsin, as general sales manager. He remained in Green Bay until 1972, when he was appointed to the post of general sales manager of WMT-TV in Cedar Rapids, Iowa.

He left WMT-TV to enter the management consulting and sales

motivation field for a couple of years, returning to active broadcast management in 1981 with KCRG–TV in Cedar Rapids.

Oetken returned to his hometown of Louisville in 1986 after being named general sales manager for WLKY-TV. He is involved in a number of industry (Kentucky Broadcasters Association, TVB) and service organizations (Kiwanis, Salvation Army, United Way, and others).

Public Interest: It Starts from the Inside

JIM OETKEN

Most of us think of the public interest in strictly external terms. We think of the service broadcasting performs in our communities, giving organizations and those in need access to almost everyone in our radio and television coverage area.

If we really are licensed to serve in the public interest, we have a great opportunity, while sharing with others in private industry our efforts to make a profit, to use our potential to reach huge masses of people in a constructive and positive way.

You may already sense a "do-gooder" theme to this piece, so it may be appropriate to explain why that is. Most of us were a little idealistic when we were young.

I wanted to save the world, so I chose psychology and sociology as a double major in college. What do you do with that kind of major? You (1) teach, assuming you are willing to get several more graduate degrees; (2) become a social worker, assuming you are willing to get several more degrees; or (3) get into broadcasting. I chose (3), got into broadcasting, and am still trying to save the world.

If we get into the broadcasting business because of "outside stuff"— the ability to reach huge numbers of people, influencing decisions that cause positive changes in our communities—we begin to realize that we can do very little acting alone. So this writing has to do with "inside stuff."

How do we get all, or most, of our associates at a radio or television station to share the vision we may have for better ways to serve public interest? I believe that most people who go to work in broadcasting have more than an average service orientation. There are a lot of "do-gooders" or "save the world" types among us, and not just in management.

I also believe that we want to work for a winning organization. That does not always mean the most profitable, but it's amazing how much direct relationship exists in most markets between strong local news and public service image and number one ratings, usually leading to high profit over the long haul.

If we somehow capitalize on the school spirit that young people bring to their jobs—kids who wore the school sweater, went to the games, and felt loyal to their high school or college—and let them know how our "team" at work has a vision, a mission, something bigger than anyone of us as an individual, we can harness some of that youthful energy and enthusiasm. And it will spread to our senior employees.

At our television station, the ABC affiliate in Louisiville, we have 105 people employed to help us serve "inside the public interest." Our management team consists of a small handful of people who set direction and policy. How effectively we serve our community is based largely on: (1) how well we choose, train, and motivate the rest of our employees, and (2) how well we communicate what we're trying to do and define their part of the plan.

For example, in the next few weeks we will be working on a number of projects:

1. A meeting with the Salvation Army to discuss a unique fund-raising plan for their annual Christmas campaign, using financial resources from viewers, advertisers, and the station.

2. A promotion with the local symphony orchestra to finalize plans for commissioning local composers/musicians to create some original music for our news open and close, with funds being used to promote attendance at the orchestra concerts.

3. Meeting with a local charitable organization (Kosair Crippled Children's Hospital) to discuss a possible telethon and other fund-raising possibilities.

4. Follow-up with local Junior Achievement officials on a new television campaign, coordinating with other stations in the market, and providing over $5,000 worth of public service time to Junior Achievement.

These are current activities, probably typical of a television or radio station's daily or weekly involvement in groups and organizations who approach us to help their visibility in the market. I think we serve them well. We serve them better when we involve most of our employees in the service we provide.

We have provided telephone training to all our employees in the past few months with a little help from our friends at "Ma Bell." People wanted it, enjoyed it, and appreciated it. Most important, it has caused some positive improvement in the way our people answer phone calls from our viewers and advertisers.

We have offered ratings seminars, conducted by several of our sales staff. Traffic, promotion, production, and news people attended, and said they learned a lot.

We have regular meetings with all our people to answer questions, explain rating trends, and announce programming or personnel plans. They've been well received, and well worth the time.

Our station is an exciting place to work right now. Why? Because we believe in the public interest, but we think it starts from the *inside*. It starts by involving all the people who provide the service, letting them share the vision, the enthusiasm, and the glory.

Broadcasting can be fun. That's what attracts many people into the business. Sometimes it's no more glamorous than cleaning up after the elephants in the Ringling Brothers Circus (although both are show business), but we often miss an opportunity to admit to applicants and new employees that it can, and should, be fun. The fun is necessary to break the tension and help build the teamwork we need. When people can laugh together, for example, they can generally support each other in stress situation and make it bearable.

Recently a reporter with a local newspaper called me and asked a few questions about condom advertising on television. He had called to determine how we in our business felt about the public interest being served by either accepting or rejecting contraceptive advertising in light of the recent AIDS concerns.

My wife and I had just moved from a twelve-story condo into a house, so my mind was on condos, not condoms. The interview went something like this:

Reporter: "I'd like to talk to you a few minutes about condoms."

Jim: "Fine ... I've been using one for about six months" (thinking he said "condos").

Reporter: "You have? For six months?"

Jim: "Yes, and we've enjoyed it."

Reporter: "Are you continuing to use it?"

Jim: "No, I'm getting into a larger unit ... the other one was getting too small for me."

Reporter: "Good grief! Do you think they should be allowed to advertise?"

Jim: "Why not? With television, they can show how roomy they are, show them with people actually in them ... it's an effective way to market them, don't you think?"

Reporter: "Yes, I suppose.... Well, thanks for a very candid interview. Good afternoon."

Jim: "Good afternoon, and you're welcome."

We do have fun, and sometimes extend that spirit of fun to our extended family—our listeners/viewers, our customers/clients, and most importantly, our employees/associates.

We used to think of cable operators as our competitors. In a sense, they are. In other ways, they are partners in our efforts to market our programming effectively to our various target audiences. We are now starting to call on cable managers throughout our coverage area—about fifty of them—to see if we can do anything to improve the quality of our service to their subscribers. If it's successful, we have established a Win-Win relationship with someone previously thought of as the "Enemy."

Why shouldn't we "woo" the cable industry? Over 50 percent of our viewers have chosen to pay for cable television, so that it is no longer a fad. If we can learn more about the cable operator and customers, we can better serve 50 percent of our audience, since they are the same people.

We need more and better research to find out how *all* of our audience perceives our service to the community. Our "report card" needs to be qualitative as well as quantitative. The rating book tells us how many people watch or listen, but additional research is needed to tell us why, and what additional information and entertainment our potential audience wants.

It seems to me that there's good news and bad news out there. The bad news (don't we always do that first?) is that we are nowhere close to living up to our public-interest potential in the electronic media.

The good news is that we're trying, we're getting better, and most of us are realizing more each day that it starts from the *inside,* and we will only reach our public interest potential when it becomes a project of the entire station.

Amen.

OTHER VIEWS

14

WOMEN'S GROWING PUBLIC INTEREST ROLE

The following speech, given by Ward L. Quaal to the National Conference of the American Women in Radio and Television in Albuquerque, New Mexico on October 18, 1980, represents yet another area of the broadcasters' public-interest spectrum.

Quaal, like other broadcast leaders from small communities to huge megalopolises, has recognized the need for total involvement in the community served. In many cases it is the local family that is served, and in others, the spectrum extends beyond broadcasting to other areas of social significance.

Many broadcasters have discovered a void in a particular area and rushed in to help fill that void. In Quaal's case, his leadership has taken many forms, both local and national. The following speech is presented as an example of how broadcasters serve by speaking out at various forums other than their own, lending their credibility and stature to further the public interest. We might also note here as a general observation that for many broadcasters in small communities and large, speaking in public is considered an essential part of the public-interest obligation.

About the Author

Ward L. Quaal is president of the Ward L. Quaal Company, a management consulting company to the communications industry. He is the retired president of WGN Continental Broadcasting Company, Chicago (WGN Tribune Broadcasting Company) and still serves as a management consultant.

Upon his graduation from the University of Michigan in 1941, he joined WGN. After serving as an officer in the U.S. Navy (1942–1945), he rejoined WGN as special assistant to the general manager. From 1949 to 1952 Quaal, on leave of absence from WGN, became executive director of the Clear Channel Broadcasting Service, Washington, D.C. He joined the Crosley Broadcasting Corporation in 1952, becoming vice president and general manager of Crosley's broadcasting properties in 1953. He returned to WGN as vice president and general manager in 1956, and was elected WGN president in 1965.

Ward Quaal has served Presidents Truman, Kennedy, Johnson, and Reagan on various commissions and task forces. He has been awarded five honorary doctorates from colleges and universities. He was elected president of Broadcast Pioneers and served on its Board of Directors from 1962 to 1973. Among the awards he has received are the Freedom Medal from the Freedom Foundation, the Distinguished Service Award from the National Association of Broadcasters, and the IBA Illinois Broadcaster of the year.

He co-authored *Broadcast Management* (Hastings House, 1968) with Leo A. Martin. A second edition was published in 1976 with co-author James A. Brown. A third edition will be published in 1988.

Women's Role in Broadcasting

WARD L. QUAAL

This is a most pleasant experience for me to be here with you today.

I have followed closely, and I want to add with profound respect, your great growth since your splendid organization was formed in 1951. I have been with you almost from the very beginning, my first talk to an AWRT group being in 1952 in New York City.

Indeed, as I was preparing a few notes for my visit with you today, I checked my business records over the years and my schedule of appearances before various industry groups, and I find that this is my ninth visit to a meeting of American Women in Radio and Television.

Now, before I flatter myself thinking that I have had nine separate invitations to address you across the length and breadth of this land, I must qualify my enthusiasm, thinking that your invitations may have gone to others, but your long-time friend always agrees to "show up."

I would like to think that you have invited me here today because you have reviewed my record in broadcast management and you have found that over a career that spans forty years in this profession, with the last thirty in management, I have given many opportunities to women in all possible areas of station operations and administration, and I have never been disappointed in their vast contributions to my companies.

While I think my record is a good one in support of key assignments and overall breath of opportunities for women in broadcasting, we are not here to talk about my humble contributions, but about *yours*, and what your fine group can do to contribute, not just to yourselves and to your very worthy and highly respected industry organization, but to the total profession of broadcasting.

I should like to stress that one of the reasons I have always been happy to address the American Women in Radio and Television in local, regional, and national sessions, is that you are a professional body. You knew your purpose when you started in 1951, and you have never departed from that platform, namely, to demonstrate to our broadcasting industry and to the allied arts, the limitless talents of women in any and all areas of our great profession.

May I say that whatever you do in your total program in the months and years to come, never depart from the professionalism that you have pursued so religiously and so effectively. It is a hallmark of quality that should never escape you, and nothing, absolutely nothing, should be employed to distract your basic premise for being an organization in our industry.

From a membership of less than 40 persons in 1951, you are now 3,000 strong with sixty chapters throughout the nation. Your good efforts bear fruit each and every day of the year as we see more and more women employed in more and more areas of broadcasting and many advancing to the very top in operations of all sizes and all geographical locations.

I think that it is interesting to note the gains that have been made. The FCC industry trend report for 1979 shows that women are continuing to make steady gains in the higher-paying positions. For example, of more than 114,000 full-time employees in the FCC's top four job categories, almost 24,000 or 21 percent were for women.

Further, tabulations show that women now hold 22 percent of manager and director positions, 24 percent of the basic professional assignments, 8.3 percent of the technicians' jobs, and 30.7 percent of the sales positions.

These figures are not surprising to me, especially insofar as they note the wide range of activities of women. With my long experience in broadcasting, I have not known a single position that a woman could not handle just as well as a man. In this industry of ours, I have been in every possible capacity from student announcer while in high school in northern Michigan, a part-time commercial announcer over WJR, Detroit, when I was a student at the University of Michigan, to my becoming general manager and later president of WGN Continental properties across the nation. In all this activity, in all phases of broadcasting, I have never known an activity I have pursued in our profession that could not have been handled by the women within our industry. Surely, you could have handled any of my varied responsibilities, and handled them very well, and perhaps, much better!

Today, it is readily apparent that more women than men are study-ing broadcasting in our colleges and universities throughout the na-tion. Through your good efforts of AWRT, you have encouraged youngsters, and they realize there is hope, that there are opportunities and challenges ahead in this great profession in which you and I have the good fortune to participate.

Your very active Washington, D.C., chapter is headed by one of the finest practitioners in the field of law. Of course, I refer to Linda Cincoitta.

In addition to her vast contributions, and they have been numerous to AWRT, Linda is the incoming president of the Federal Commu-nications Bar Association, founded by my dear friend and mentor, the late Louis Goldsborough Caldwell, the first general counsel of the old Federal Radio Commission, predecessor of today's FCC.

One doesn't have to think too long to realize what it means to our young people to see a fine woman such as Linda gaining recognition daily as one of the outstanding lawyers in the nation's capital in her capacity with Arent, Fox, Kinter, Plotkin & Kahn, now having gained such respect from the legal fraternity in Washington that she is to head the FCC Bar Association.

As we address ourselves to the great growth in the stature of AWRT and the role of women in broadcasting and communications, in gen-eral, we would be remiss if we didn't mention Katherine Meyer Gra-ham, present chairperson of the American Newspaper Publisher's Association and chairperson of the Washington Post Company, in-cluding its vast broadcast holdings. Then there is Jean Auman, the incumbent national president of the Society of Professional Journal-ism, Sigma Delta Chi.

Through the broadcasting industry, from coast to coast, we have seen the fruits of the efforts of American Women in Radio and Tel-evision in pursuing its aggressive program in elevating the status of women. Of course, we who believe in the participation of more and more women in key roles in broadcasting can never be satisfied.

Bear in mind that women can do what a man can do if a person's talents are truly and effectively "harnessed." Success will come through proper attitudes and application. Women must move for-ward to develop their talents, to be more aggressive and to maximize whatever abilities they have in their never-ending "march to the top."

In conversations with your conference chair, Mary Noskin, and with Brenda Ashworth, as program chairperson of this conference, I have noted the underscoring of several subjects and I should like to deal briefly with them here.

I feel that women can become viable candidates for middle and upper-level management positions throughout the entire broadcasting industry. To rise from one position in broadcasting to a higher level, it is going to take initiative, industry, and really *quality* more than assertiveness. To compete with men for the same post, women are going to have to be just as aggressive and just as determined as men. We have already talked about the fact that women can do any job that a man can do in our profession. I find that all too many women become comfortably ensconced in a lower-level post in broadcasting and do not seek higher positions either within that same company or elsewhere in the industry. Men are far more assertive, far more demanding of opportunities, and of course, some of this comes from the fact that in many homes, men are the sole supplier of the family needs, from a monetary standpoint. Also, I have found that many women do not take the time to look into available positions to find out what the needs and the demands of that post really are. I think if interest were shown, many more opportunities would open for women. Briefly, I should like to tell the story of a young lady currently employed by WBBM Radio, Chicago. Her name is Linda Muskin. I have never had the pleasure of meeting her, but she has the *right idea*! She is moving forward by demanding more of herself and showing management she is prepared for bigger things.

Only a few years ago she was a fledgling trainee at WBBM News. She handled minor production assignments; then she was elevated to top responsibility for certain segments of time on this all news/sports station. Her next step was as a writer and on-the-air news personality. She kept advancing, kept doing a superior job in every area of activity, but still she wasn't satisfied. She wants to go to the "top," the very "top," so she asked to become a trainee in sales, as she feels that area is the "entrance gate" to the top command post. At some companies, that is the final stepping stone to the "promised land." Linda is doing mighty well where she is now, and I am betting on her to finish first, first in every respect. She has the drive, the competitive spirit that I like to see in our women in broadcasting. Really, she is showing the way!

I am not saying here now that getting into the sales department is the course to pursue to anything in the higher levels of life in a broadcasting property. In my own case, I have long felt that a person's ability, male or female, in one department or another, determined whether or not that individual was going to go to bigger things at the company. In the way I have done business over the years, everyone in every department has an opportunity to move forward if they have the talents to go to a higher level in the company. It is a matter of record, of course, that in many segments of our broadcasting industry, the sales route is the most popular one to follow if one is to seek an opportunity for more middle or upper management assignments.

We have talked a little bit here about the psychology or what it takes to become management material. In short, you have to have it in you to want to go to the top! My advice would be to set your goal and then get about attaining it. Always remember what one of the famous advertising agency giants of all time, the late and great Leo Burnett, said about one's future. Addressing a group of young people at our mutual alma mater, the University of Michigan, Ann Arbor, Mr. Burnett said "reach for the stars, you may not get a handful, but you won't get a fistful of mud, either!" Yes, set your goals and set them high!

With further reference to the psychology of what it takes to become management material, I think that you women, upon taking broadcast assignments, should stress to management that you are interested in advancing in the company and that you want to know more about every phase of the company and its total operations. This tells top management that you are there, planning for the future, not just someone who finds out the working hours, holiday schedule, and the vacation periods available.

Of course, I want to stress here that I know of no better course to take to succeed, especially in our competitive industry, than to put forth the maximum in *good hard work*! Maybe there is something wrong with me, but in every post I have occupied at the lowest possible level, as a management trainee, at middle management, as general manager of huge companies, and as president of a national entity with numerous subsidiaries, I have never become accustomed to the eight-hour day or to the four-week vacation. Indeed, I would have to think a long time if I could come forth with many success stories about the men and women who "call it quits" at 5 P.M.

If you ever read the book entitled *Working* by Studs Terkel of Chicago, you know my hours, and I still keep them after a long time at the top in broadcast management. I should like to recall here one of our profession's greatest executives, Dr. Frank Stanton, long-time president of CBS. If you wanted to talk to Frank at his office you could reach him there at 8 in the morning and until 7:55 P.M. He did leave at 8 o'clock to go home for dinner. By the way, if you would have liked to talk to him on Saturday morning, he was there from 8 A.M. to 1 P.M. He didn't do that just to *get to the top*; he *stayed there* by doing exactly that!

This is not an easy business. Our opportunities in broadcasting were made possible by the great pioneers of this industry. They did not sit around and work the proverbial "banking hours"; they struggled and produced. You will find today in the leading halls of this industry that the workers and the "doers," those who are performing to advance broadcasting and the allied arts, are still there at night, long after the crowd has gone home for dinner.

Mary Noskin and Brenda asked me about the skills, talents, and the education necessary for persons to become potential broadcast management. We have touched upon some of these areas, but above all, I want to stress the importance of our young people first getting a good liberal arts education, and hopefully, while matriculating at a college or university, courses in broadcasting will be available. Where opportunities present themselves for actual experience in radio and television, educational or commercial, while in college, that is a bonus for which every student should be grateful.

As to talents, no two people are alike in any profession. Therefore, it is essential that a person seeking to rise to the broadcast management level learn as much as possible about all phases of a broadcasting operation from the cost of meeting the payroll to the most complex engineering needs. You can go to the top and function effectively only if you know what the people below you in the organization have to do in their day-to-day responsibility. I have always taken pride, if I may be a bit presumptuous, to state that I could face my employees, anytime, anywhere, in any situation, and they knew very well that I could do what they could do. Of course, I came along in broadcasting's early years and therefore, I had many more opportunities than manifest themselves now, although today a person is paid for it and that wasn't true in my starting years! One final thought about education. I do feel that it is essential that a person achieves the equivalent of a four-year college program, whether this is done by age twenty-two or forty-two, by regular hours and months of attendance at colleges and universities, or via night school. I feel any formal education beyond those four years should be taken after hours, as time permits, because I feel that actual broadcasting experience is the finest academic laboratory a person can have to achieve goals in our profession.

Many companies are now giving special attention to the training of mid-level managers to become upper-level management. Where you see these programs in force, AWRT should thank and congratulate those station owners and administrators for their foresightedness and work with them and help them, and perhaps this could lead also to some prudential and productive achievements in female recruiting. Obviously, it is in the interest of American Women in Radio & Television to encourage all broadcasting properties to do this. Again, the approach should be on a *local* basis in a course of strengthening your ties with individual radio and television stations in your midst. Always bear in mind, in anything you want to accomplish, it is best to do it *locally*. That is where you are known; that is where you have your strength and that is where you will finally make the high marks and win!

I hope that each one of your women will always bear in mind that you are most effective when you make these presentations to your fellow broadcasters as the true professionals you are. There is no need to bring in outside entities to help you. We, who are in management, recognize and respect the vast contributions that women are making in the broadcast arts. You are one of us, a big part of us, and you are helping to write broadcasting's success stories everyday of the week at every station in the nation. Always retain your *professionalism.*

Now I should like to address myself to the matter of recruiting women for management positions. This could be accomplished in many ways, but we have to start on a modest scale and move forward from that point. As many of you know, I am in profound respect of the truly great performance we in our industry are receiving from Vince Wasilewski and his fine team at the National Association of Broadcasters.

At this point, I want to commend Vince and his staff especially for their dedicated efforts on behalf of women and minorities. As you know, the "clearinghouse" regarding employment is functioning well and it will have an even greater contribution to make in the near future.

I have had several discussions with NAB officials on what might be done to assist AWRT in a program of recruiting women for key management assignments. Needless to say, we cannot put the NAB in a position of a "recruiter" or as a "job placement service." On the other hand, I do know that the NAB is anxious to be of help in whatever practical manner can be devised.

Meanwhile, may I suggest to the women of this great organization that you consider a "test" program whereby the key chapters in Washington, D.C., Chicago, New York, and Los Angeles begin this recruiting program by placing in charge on a full-, or even a part-time basis, one or more of your members at each location to assemble and make available to management recruiters information on the many women in our midst who aspire to "bigger things" in broadcasting and the allied arts.

I realize the expense involved in such an undertaking, and maybe the "tests" should be made in just one of those markets, preferably New York.

The individual "in charge" will have to take the time to get to know those persons who engage in recruiting positions seeking qualified management personnel. That individual cannot sit in an office and wait for the phone to ring or to be looking forward to tomorrow's mail. It has to be a case of personal contact, and when that individual does make contact, she is going to have to be armed with information on those who aspire to higher levels in our profession.

While I do not know what the NAB will be prepared to do in this area, I know that Vince Wasilewski and his colleagues will do, as they have all along, everything possible to aid this enterprising program which you women should and must have as you move ahead to become a still greater factor in our rapidly growing industry.

Now that I have told you how good you are, I am now going to give a brief lecture.

Briefly speaking, the industry that you and I love so very much, needs help, and needs it now! There is nothing that you could do that would be more productive to your future and to that of other women who will follow you in the broadcasting arts than for you to assume a very aggressive, a very formidable role in political action, in legislation and in regulation, yes, to help those of us who have long worked in these vineyards to supply the "life blood" of the business of broadcasting in all of its countless new technological manifestations.

The Washington Chapter has been recognized, and properly so, in my earlier remarks. It constitutes an excellent nucleus on which to launch an effort in this important and vital area of broadcasting on the federal front. There is no limit to the contributions women in broadcasting can make to this area which is taking more and more time on the part of industy leadership from year to year to protect the interest of broadcasting and the people for whom we are licensed to serve.

Let us never forget that we have in these United States the greatest system of broadcasting yet devised. Regardless of what our critics may have to say, there is nothing, absolutely nothing, anywhere in the world that can compare to the American system of broadcasting and that which it contributes to the people in this lovely land. Beyond the role of AWRT in the federal area, state activity in all our fifty states can be handled appropriately and effectively by employing the patterns established by the National Association of Broadcasters. There is work to be done to defend broadcasting and to enhance its posture for superior service to the public in every state of the nation. In that regard, each one of us who has the good fortune to be in broadcasting should never forget our prime responsibility and that is to protect with all the vigor within us the precious First Amendment to the Constitution of the United States.

Many of us have worked over countless periods from time to time on this area of responsibility on both federal and state levels. Women have been active, but they can do much more, and what a great role this would be for AWRT.

I learned a long time ago that when women make up their minds to something in which they believe, they move forward with intensity and with innate sincerity, and they seem to be so successful, and above all, let me say I have noted this in the legislative area. I have seen some campaigns conducted by women in the legislative arena where their performance was truly outstanding! Generally, you are more tenacious and furthermore, you are so effective in developing from politicians and from government leadership a degree of deference that is not always present when these same people are dealing with men in their midst.

With sixty chapters of AWRT across the country, your members, working in conjunction with the fifty state broadcasting associations could contribute vastly to the success we must have in the state capitols of our nation.

I hope that at your next national meeting, and at the approaching sessions of your various chapters, you would place this thought high on the agenda. There is no limit to the height of the success to which you can lay claim. The future is yours! I believe in you! I just want to make sure that I am there with you as a fellow broadcaster as I see your accomplishments mount and mount over the months and years to come!

Finally, as I close with very special gratitude for your courtesy in having me with you today, I thought I might quote some brief remarks of two good friends of mine. The first one is a brilliant federal judge in Chicago, the Honorable Abraham Lincoln Marovitz. He was so touched one evening as we were paying tribute to a dedicated Chicagoan, that he left the scene of the dinner and composed some beautiful and very proper lines. He was so moved by the occasion that he could not read that which he had before him, so he asked me to do so. I memorized his thoughts and upon conclusion of the dinner, I came forth with his quotation.

> Life is sweet because of the friends we have made and of the things which in common we share. We want to live on, not because of ourselves, but because of the people who care. It's the giving and doing for somebody else upon that life's future depends. For the joy of the world, when you sum it all up, is found in the making of friends.

Unfortunately, I never had the opportunity to meet the author of the next quotation. He lived considerably ahead of our time. I am referring now to Henry David Thoreau who left behind some truly wonderful thoughts that I repeat frequently. At his beloved Waldon Pond in Massachusetts, Thoreau wrote:

> I know of no more comforting fact than the unquestioned ability of man to elevate his life through conscious endeavor.
>   Oh, it is something to be able to paint a picture or carve a statue,

or to make a few objects beautiful, but it is far more glorious to paint and to carve the very atmosphere and the medium through which we look, which morally we can do.

To effect the quality of the day that is the very highest of the arts!

Thank you so much and my best wishes to each of you.

15

NO FAULT PUBLIC INTEREST

As one whose career in advertising relates closely to broadcasting, Joseph Ostrow's concern about public interest revolves around the criticism that broadcasters have received over the years for many social problems. As he puts it, "from the decay of cities to the decay of teeth," the promotion of violence, "the lack of intellectual stimulation," widespread criticism is directed at television. Neither are the realities of television met by intellectual analyses, which might be accurate but remain too narrow. Statistics as well add little insight. Counting the hours watching television or listening to the radio could be matched by time "wasted" waiting for elevators, planes, and other things—or watching water boil.

Television as a public art has the capacity to lead, universalize social developments, spot a trend or kill it, as well as assist in the rebirth of dormant phenomena. It is an image of what is or is becoming. Those who accuse television of creating social problems do so because television is a convenient whipping boy for what really exists around us. Television is not the problem, we are.

One might extend Ostrow's observations by reminding the critics that creating the impression that television is the cause of social problems instead of a mirror for them, is to overlook its potential for serving the public interest. If television can be used more effectively to make us look at ourselves, perhaps it will have best served the public interest. And it often does just that.

About the Author

Joseph W. Ostrow's experience at Young & Rubicam, New York, began in 1955 following a brief stay with the W. R. Simmons Research

Company. He began at Young & Rubicam in the Research Department and moved to the Media Department in 1958. His responsibilities have covered both media buying and planning, including direct work with almost every Y & R account. His is currently executive vice president and director of communications services, a member of the New York Executive Committee of the agency, and one of the U.S. company's Board of Directors.

His industry activities include being past president of the Media Directors Council, past vice president of advertising information services, past chairman of the Traffic Audit Bureau, vice chairman of the Four A's Media Policy Committee, member of the Board and Executive Committee of the NOAB, co-chairman of the IRTS Industry/Faculty College Conference and member of the Board of the Audit Bureau of Circulations.

He writes for several trade publications including *Advertising Age* and *Marketing & Media Decisions*. He has lectured at Cornell, New York University, and the Annenberg School of Communications.

He attended Cornell and New York University. He is married with three children and lives in Manhattan.

A No Fault Perspective on Public Interest

JOSEPH W. OSTROW

I do remember a life before television when broadcast was not sight or motion but simply sound. In a way it was a time when broadcasting may have had fewer limitations in what it was able to achieve. With the deft movement of the "sound men," we were transported from home to the planet Krypton or on a trip down the Mississippi with Huck Finn. The spectrum of things that radio delivered was limited only by one's own imagination. If the "FBI in Peace and War" had a scene in which gangsters were machine-gunning each other in the street, little if anything was heard about how this would distort the perspective of America's youth. "The Romance of Helen Trent" was not viewed as immoral or about to cause the downfall of the family. In fact, the family was expected to set its own standards and was responsible for its own behavior.

Contrary to the relatively "laissez-faire" feelings about radio, television is depicted by many public-spirited individuals as being at the heart of the decay in American society. There is probably no need to identify the vast number and variety of criticisms that are laid at television's doorstep. In fact, I won't even differentiate between the criticisms that relate to programming and those that are directed toward commercials. For while there are differences between these criticisms, the main thrust is generally the same. It deals essentially with the word "excess." There is too much television viewing just as there are too many television commercials. The tone of the programming and commercials is viewed by some as demeaning to the levels of intelligence in society, and yet somehow they are also provocative in terms of their influence upon people's life-styles. It's quite puzzling, incidentally, how something that is so far beneath the intelligence of the population can at the same time be thought to have such a great influence on it.

Many have also laid at the doorstep of television broadcasting and commercials the blame for very specific societal maladies. These range from the decay of cities to the decay of children's teeth. These indictments include a belief that television promotes violence and/or (you can take your choice) promotes the development of apathy toward violence. Criticism also includes the lack of intellectual stimulation offered by television and calls for greater use of television for educational purposes. There are many who also decry the loss of the great television dramas of the past. They mourn "Studio One" and "Playhouse 90" and totally ignore how far television has come in a total sense. Few of these critics choose to recall that among the Emmy winners for 1948 was a show entitled "Mike Stokey's Pantomine Quiz" and the top personality was Shirley Dinsdale and her puppet "Judy Splinters."

I find it to be societally irrelevant to venture into the physiological never-never land of Marshal McLuhan. For to me a hot medium or a cold medium or even the tribulation of a society fails miserably in attempting to face the realities that are television. These discussions which intellectualize phenomena, while perhaps correct, ignore the main issues and fail to provide anything other than a very narrow perspective.

I also think that statistics add little to key issues. I'm tired of hearing about the 14,000 or 14,000,000 hours of television that kids will view before they reach the age of twenty-one. I'm sure that if there were good radio statistics, one could construct similarly frightening numbers about radio listening during the 1930s and 1940s. We could probably also construct some horrifying statistics about the amount of time "wasted" waiting for trains, planes, buses, and elevators, or the total time spent doing crossword puzzles or even waiting for water to boil.

Television is a public art that allows our society to see it now—to see it as it is, as it was, or as it could be. It is an internalized reflection of society. It is no different in many ways from Shakespeare's reflection of his own age even when viewed through period pieces that dealt with times other than the Shakespearean years.

Television certainly does have the capacity to lead society as it has demonstrated many time. Its role is not in the form of dramatic long-range breakthroughs or huge quantum leaps. It does, however, possess the qualities to spread out new societal developments and to universalize them in an almost instantaneous fashion. It has the capability to take an emerging and developing taste and spread it from coast to coast, from hamlet to major metropolitan center. It can and often does spot a trend ready to be born and take it from infancy to adulthood in a matter of weeks or months. It can also help in the rebirth of phenomena that had existed and were dormant. This type of rediscovery often brings with it an evolutionary aspect whereby the old phenomenon, in its relaunch, is being updated to current circumstances and conditions. In a most obvious fashion, television hypos fads. It brings them to their peak very quickly and often to their demise almost as fast.

An extension of television's capability to hypo and kill trends is manifest within the medium itself. Television programs are themselves subject to a short moment of possible glory and a high mortality rate. Many, pushed by impatient networks, clients, and agencies, are killed before they have a chance to develop audience loyalties. These often premature deaths reflect an attempt on the part of all concerned to read viewer reactions quickly and cut losses with equal speed. In many ways, therefore, television is its own greatest victim.

Now to anyone who views society and its component groups it should be clear that there has always been a segment of the population that didn't like the then current life-style. In a nontelevision era these people might have blamed leaders in society, government, or politics for setting the tone that lead to these patterns of life that they found to be abhorrent. Today, however, they have a very convenient whipping boy. Television has often become the focus of their discontent with trends in society.

However, to suggest that television is causative is absolute and utter nonsense. Television is basically a mirror image of society; what it is and what it is becoming. A television program that is out of touch with the current life-style cannot and does not succeed. Television reflects what exists on our streets, on our farms, in our air, and under our waters.

If we were to force-feed a change in television's programming, the major results might be a reduction in television viewing and even more rapid turnover in programming as the medium scrambled to try to maintain respectable rating levels. It would produce severe injury to one of the most magnificent forms of communication ever invented.

If there are faults in television, it is because there are faults in society. If children watch too much television or the wrong kinds of programs, let us not place television "in loco parentis"; let's rather educate parents as to what their function should be. Certainly there is a need for a balance between cartoons and "Sesame Street." And direct experience as well, I might add. But that balance should be constructed as a result of parental or educational efforts rather than a grand vizier of television telling parents what's right or wrong with their children. Furthermore, beyond the children's issues is the question of overall programming controls.

I, for one, believe that today's television medium, with its free and paid cable, VCR's, access channels, Direct Broadcast Satellite, and so on, is the best of all possible media situations. It is the epitome of democracy in action where choice is there for almost every taste. The consumer marketplace turns its dials and makes its preferences known, a circumstance that might cause gray hairs for programmers and distributors, but one which gives the medium an opportunity to fulfill its total range of potentials.

Finally, therefore, television is not a cause, it is an effect. It is not a developer, it is a hypo. It is not the problem, we are.

16

NOT-FOR-PROFITS'
ACCESS

The problem as Edgar Vovsi sees it is that there are more not-for-profit organizations clamoring for airtime than there is time available. This creates a highly competitive situation, but the chances of gaining airtime can be enhanced by presenting professional quality material to the broadcaster. Still there are misunderstandings, poor planning, impossible competition created by popular programming, and the possibility of being assigned a time slot when there is little or no audience.

He states that broadcasting is market driven where "the public's interest is dictated by the public." But all is not lost. The expansion of cable television and radio talk shows, for example, provide opportunities for the not-for-profits to gain the audience's attention provided the message is professionally attractive. Not-for-profits, unlike the broadcasters they approach, often know little about their potential audiences.

Vovsi is aware of the broadcaster's power to influence. He concludes that the use of the media is not in the public's interest because the broadcasters must broadcast in their own interest. And only the public can care for its own interest.

If the public interest is to be served, the broadcaster and the not-for-profits must work together. The broadcaster should understand the constraints under which the latter must operate.

About the Author

Edgar A. Vovsi has been the executive vice president of the American Heart Association, Illinois Affiliate, since 1980. In this position he serves as the chief executive officer of a statewide association that generates some $2.75 million in annual income through a corps of volunteer leadership supported by twenty-five professional and thirty-two support staff. During his tenure, the association's income has increased by 54 percent.

Vovsi's prior positions include director of administrative services of the Greater Los Angeles Affiliate of the American Heart Association (1974–1980); associate director, California Heart Association (1968–1974); executive director, Alameda Country Heart Association, Oakland, California (1964–1968); director of public information, Illinois Heart Association (1959–1964); city editor, *Daily Times*, Pekin, Illinois; reporter, *Journal Star*, Peoria, Illinois (1958–1959).

He holds a B.S. degree in journalism from Bradley University, Peoria, Illinois (1959), an M.A. in history from Holy Names College, Oakland, California (1973), and a certificate from the Managerial Policy Institute of the University of Southern California Graduate School of Business Administration (1978).

Among the organizations he has served in are: American Heart Association National Staff Society (1964–present); American Heart Association Senior Management Advisory Group (1982–1985); American Society of Association Executives; Bradley University National Alumni Board of Directors (1982–present).

Vovsi served with the U.S. Air Force from 1952 to 1956. He was born in Riga, Latvia, in 1933.

Not-for-Profits Access the Airwaves: Addressing the Public's Interest

EDGAR A. VOVSI

Armed with a background rooted in journalism, I am not so naive that I cannot accept the fact that the media, broadcast as well as print, represents businesses established to generate a profit for owners and investors. Profit margins and return on investment vary, I suppose, from facility to facility and from ownership to ownership, so the contribution of free air time involves much more than public access and public interest. It involves hard-line business issues—dollars and cents, if you will.

It should be obvious to all of us who view the broadcasting industry from the outside that the financial success of a radio or television station depends upon the sale of time at a maximum dollar level commensurate with demand. It should be equally obvious that the greatest return on investment must be generated during prime listening or viewing hours. Giving that valuable time away just does not make good business sense.

Yet despite the ability, no doubt, to sell that time, broadcasters do give it away, and yet those in the not-for-profit sector continuously clamor for more, displaying an attitude that free prime time access is their birthright. I think that the crux of the problem may well be that there are more takers out there than there are potential givers, and that there can never be enough available free prime time to feed the appetites of the multitude of not-for-profits.

Let's face it, I'm thrilled if my organization's thirty-second PSA finds a slot preceding the 6 o'clock news. I envy the United Way's relationship with the National Football League, and the promos it receives during every NFL telecast. But those things don't happen by chance; they don't happen without design. The lesson that not-for-profits must learn is that they must develop creative and innovative ways to assure their messages being aired.

Since the majority of not-for-profits depend upon broadcasters' contributing public service time, the competition for that time is overwhelming, if not brutal. I don't know how a given program or public service director allocates PSA time, but I do know that if that person is committed to your cause or issue, your chances of having your message heard are greatly enhanced. If your PSA's are professionally produced, entertaining and informative, you have again increased your chances of having them aired. The personal involvement of a station's owner or management team on behalf of a cause lends that cause a level of support which would never otherwise be affordable.

PSA's, however, are not the only air time access available to not-for-profits. Among the sector's other approaches to the broadcast media are co-sponsored special events, talk and community affairs programming, news, and features.

Co-sponsored events give not-for-profits access to an enormous amount of air time, primarily the time the station devotes to promoting the event. Too many times, unfortunately, the co-sponsoring station seems to think that the promotion of the event is where its responsibility ends, and the not-for-profit is finally left to its own devices in implementing the event. As an example, a division of my association was approached by a local radio station with a suggestion that they co-sponsor a Valentine's Day dance. The radio station began to promote the event, assigned staff to work with the association's staff to plan the event, secured the local convention center as a site, hired a band, and completed other preparations. On the evening of the event, however, radio station staff arrived to party, not to work, and bristled at the suggestion that their responsibility was to assure the success of the event, not to have a good time.

The upshot of this co-sponsorship was that the station accused the association of poor planning, of not having enough staff and volunteers in attendance to handle the crowd, and even demanded that the association's volunteer leadership terminate their staff executive vice president. The income generated at the event was withheld by the station for some five months, and when it was turned over, it contained numerous checks which had not been cashed. The association was then left to deal with the irate contributors who couldn't understand why their checks had not been cashed.

On the other hand, some co-sponsorships work beautifully. In 1986, for example, the Illinois Affiliate of the American Heart Association in cooperation with the Illinois Broadcasters Association, developed a project called "Turn on Heart Radiothon." Twelve radio stations from all corners of the state participated in the project, which serves to recruit volunteers for the association's residential campaign, while also providing air time for PSA's, physician interviews, and call-in questions from the listening public. The radio station devotes one day to the project, but can retain as much time for other local programming that it feels it needs.

So, well-planned, properly implemented co-sponsored projects can work for the good of both the not-for-profit and the broadcaster. Each must accept a share of the responsibilities for a project and then fulfill those responsibilities. When such a project is well done, the community at large is the beneficiary.

Community affairs programs which, it seems, are all scheduled early on a Saturday or Sunday afternoon opposite major-league baseball, NFL football, or NBA basketball offer another avenue for a not-for-profit to access the airwaves. Since most public affairs programs follow an interviewer-interviewee format for thirty minutes, mercifully punctuated by commercial breaks, they generate about as much excitement as watching garden-variety grass grow. I suppose that cost-wise, early Saturday or Sunday afternoon is expendable, so why increase the cost of that time with high production costs? I've always thought that the only people who tune in to this format are the relatives of the interviewee and some self-interested folks who are members of the interviewee's organization or cause and have already bought into the message. On the other hand, if the weather is wonderful or the football game is crucial, even they will probably desert.

Hard news is another avenue open to the not-for-profit. But let's face it, not-for-profits rarely generate the kind of hard news that makes the five-minute local news break on radio, or the evening television newscast. Oh sure, construction of a local Ronald McDonald House will get some local play, and the American Cancer Society's "Great American Smokeout" receives fleeting national mention, but by and large, not-for-profits have to scrape to create events that one would deem "newsworthy."

Feature stories can be generated by not-for-profits, but those lend themselves primarily to the print media and not to broadcast, unless a given television or radio station wishes to devote the time and its production facilities to developing a feature. Fortunately, many not-for-profits have available video and audio clips that can be used in the production of a broadcast feature, but local stations tend to shy away from doing half-hour public service productions that possibly entail work outside the studio setting. Unfortunately, it seems, more Pulitzer Prizes seem to be handed out to the crusading reporter exposing community graft and corruption than to the education reporter explaining that cigarette smoking causes dreaded diseases and shortens life.

Well, then, where does all of this lead? Since in marketing parlance there are so many segments of the public, what does broadcasting in the public interest really mean? I daresay that the majority of the public's interest lies in settling in for an evening of "Miami Vice," "Family Ties," prime-time wrestling, or any syndicated game show, soap opera, or MTV; or becoming tone deaf with a top-forty rocker, reliving the sounds of the 1950s and 1960s, or getting their current events from Larry King, Paul Harvey, or Dr. Toni Grant. The few who support public broadcasting are the people in our society considered to be out of the mainstream, and I have always resented the fact that PBS stations have to shill for contribution from the public to be able to stay on the air.

The name of the game today is being market driven, to be able to disect the wants, needs, and life-styles of the particular segments we want to reach, and then to feed those wants and needs. Arbitron, Nielsen, Gallup, Yankelovich, and a host of others continuously generate the demographic data, which eventually dictate what all of us see and hear. Thus, in a marketing sense, the public's interest is dictated by the public, and catered to by advertisers, program developers, and the broadcasters through whom the advertising and programming finds its final outlet.

If the marketplace does, in fact, determine what it sees and hears, one must have grave doubts about the impact a stand-alone not-for-profit PSA makes in the jungle of constant, repetitive commercial messages. Repetitive commercial overkill is obviously the Madison Avenue approach to the selling of a product, and not for profits are usually restricted, by policy, from puchasing media time or space. Faced with this dilemma, not-for-profits respond by working even harder to access what limited time is available to them. Some succeed; the majority fail. Can not-for-profits access a greater share of broadcast time? Probably not, or at least not until the public clamors for a greater amount of time being made available, or broadcasters turn their backs on potential revenue to open lucrative prime-time minutes to not-for-profits. Neither is likely to occur in the near future.

This is not to say that all is, or has to be, gloom and doom. The explosion of cable television has seen the development of special interest networks such as "Lifeline" and the Cable News Network does cover "soft" news and does present short features in fields such as health, science, and the arts. As noted earlier, local radio stations, when approached properly and with a professionally attractive package, will dedicate time for the education and edification of the listening public across demographic lines. Network "talk" radio is another accessible medium for the not-for-profit sector. The bottom line, however, still deals with who is listening or watching. The demographers know, the advertisers know, the broadcasters should know, and the not-for-profits, by and large, do not know.

It falls upon the not-for-profits to become as demographically astute as their profit-sector brethren, albeit they are getting a late start. Some not-for-profits long ago figured out this name of the game and began to move their messages into the spectrum of entertainment programming, particularly on television. Both the Heart Association and the Cancer Society were able to work with the producers of the hit sitcom, "All in the Family," which in its story line incorporated major messages related to cancer and to heart disease. One program was totally devoted to cardiopulmonary resuscitation, and probably did more to heighten public awareness of CPR than all of the community efforts that had preceded it. Other television series have tackled important social and health issues with the result of greatly heightening public awareness. I am convinced that if an antismoking campaign were launched on MTV using messages from current rock stars, the incidence of adolescent and teenage smoking in America would drop significantly.

It is scary to think of the power to influence that is inherent within the broadcast industry. The advertising agencies certainly play on that power, and so do their clients. Is the use of the broadcast media's influence in the public's interest? I don't think so, but then that's not the media's problem. That's society's problem. The public has to be able to discern the validity of messages. The public has to understand that it is looked upon as a statistic to be marketed. The public has to realize that everything it sees or hears is not necessarily the truth. The public has to realize that only the public can look out for its own best interest. The public has to accept the notion that broadcasters really broadcast in the broadcasters' interest. Don't tell me, for example, that the Christian Broadcasting Network broadcasts for anyone's interest other than its own.

Let me just take one brief glimpse at an issue which broadcasters certainly have not addressed in the public interest. Back in the "good old days" tobacco companies advertised cigarette brands over the airwaves. As the health hazards of cigarette smoking became more apparent and accepted, antismoking messages were aired as a "fairness doctrine" mandate. When the ban on broadcast cigarette advertising was issued, how did broadcasters react? Recognizing the implicit dangers to health, did broadcasters continue to promote the antismoking message? Heavens no! Antismoking PSA's were, by and large, relegated to the round file, despite the mounting evidence generated by the health industry related to the active and passive negative effects of cigarette smoke. Was it still in the public's interest to have the negative effects of smoking presented factually? Undoubtedly yes. Was it in the broadcast industry's interest to continue to promote the antismoking message? Apparently not.

I do not intend to imply that all broadcasters or broadcast organizations can be painted with the same brush. Consider the Illinois Broadcasters Association, which a number of years ago made a commitment to address the abuse of drugs in its broadest sense. In concert with a corporate sponsor, the association entered into a multiyear project aimed at driving home the antidrug message. Geared primarily to the young people of the state, the project has already addressed alcohol abuse and substance abuse and is now addressing tobacco as an addictive drug. The uniqueness of this program is that individual broadcasters make a commitment to take the message into their communities through personal appearances at clubs, youth groups, service organizations, and elsewhere. Here is an example of a positive use of the influence that the media has to isolate an important issue, and to inform and educate with the use of personalities recognizable within a given geographic area.

So it seems that public interest is not a tangible, but is in fact, a perception. It is probably safe to assume that seen from the point of view of broadcasters, the broadcasting industry operates in the public interest. It is probably just as safe to assume that from the point of view of the majority of not-for-profits, access to the airwaves is limited, and thus not in the public interest. And maybe this is the way it ought to be. By not having a guarantee to the airwaves, not-for-profits are challenged to seek unique approaches for airtime, and to develop PSA's worthy of being seen and heard. Broadcasters, on the other hand, are offered a cafeteria of information and material from which to select those they feel appropriate for transmission to their publics.

As in any other marketplace, the competitive edge will accrue to those who are a little more creative, work a little harder, do a little better followup, and maintain their media contacts better. Not-for-profits need to accept the fact that there are no guarantees when seeking airtime. Broadcasters need to understand that not-for-profits may not be as professionally astute as commercial advertisers in their attempts to access the airwaves. Serving the public's interest can only come through a cooperative effort which sees the not-for-profit understanding and accepting the needs of the broadcasters, and which sees the broadcaster understanding and accepting the constraints under which the not-for-profit functions.

It may not be the most perfect of systems, but so far it seems to be the best we've got. By being aware of each other's needs, broadcasters and not-for-profits can work together in addressing the public's interest.

SOME CONCLUDING THOUGHTS

Congress, by legislation and through the FCC, regulates the broadcasters' use of a limited public resource, the frequency spectrum. In order to obtain permission to use a frequency and have that permission renewed periodically, the broadcaster is required not only to follow technical regulations, but also to establish a record of fulfilling programmatic obligations in the public interest. The principle that the public has ownership of the spectrum as a scarce resource has been the continuing justification for federal regulation over programming.

The reality of the practice of broadcasting, however, is that once granted permission to use a frequency, the broadcaster is then able to *act* as the owner within the context of very broad regulations. Radio and television stations are sold and resold, their value generally determined by the financial success of their operation and the size of the markets they reach—the larger markets bring higher prices. The selling of a broadcast station—often referred to as "property"—has little to do with who (the public) actually owns the frequency. It has everything to do with who has access to the use of that frequency. Most often for the short and long run, the federal government has granted to the broadcaster not only the right to broadcast on a frequency, but also the right to sell the use of that frequency. This situation of the broadcaster *acting* as the owner is at the heart of the tension that exists between the FCC and the broadcaster.

Long ago, it was decided that the American system of broadcasting would be fundamentally commercial, while still recognizing the much smaller exception of public broadcasting. Like other commercial enterprises, commercial broadcasters survive by producing an acceptable level of profit. They must do so by presenting a visible (or listenable) product that attracts a public while conforming to federal standards of public interest in order to continue to act like owners of those frequencies to which they have been granted exclusive access. Thus, as a temporary "owner" (that is, exclusive user) of a frequency, the broadcaster must please the public *and* the FCC to make a profit. This is the reality of American broadcasting.

In the effort to sustain a business while satisfying FCC rules and regulations, the commercial broadcaster interprets the concept of public interest in a variety of ways as seen in the foregoing articles. Different approaches are taken to match the needs and aspirations of the public served. Sometimes the program is an investigation of a local problem; often it involves raising money for a charitable cause; or it may simply raise public consciousness about good health or safety practices through public service announcements sometimes shown during prime time, often late at night. In addition to the airing of programs, the broadcasters may involve the community itself in a project with the public appearing on camera or before the microphone. And station's staff participates at times directly in community activities.

What stands out in the preceding articles, however, is that beyond federal law and FCC regulations, the broadcaster knows that to operate a successful business means the public interest must be served. Like any another other commercial enterprise, concept of public interest has to be built into the operation if it is to succeed. Just as the bottom line is profit, so is the effective application of public interest. They go hand in hand.

Potential conflict exists between what the public is interested in and what the government perceives as good for the public interest. The broadcaster may be caught between what is seen as a reasonable judgment and what the government mandates. For example, the broadcaster can be forbidden to advertise certain products that are legally sold and advertised extensively by other media. But the government has deemed it to be in the public interest that such a ban be issued, all of which brings us to the First Amendment.

Under the jurisdiction of a representative democracy with a Constitution specifically banning government restraint of expression, the broadcaster can still be forbidden to use access to a frequency to air certain messages. This was mandated by Congress despite the fact that those messages cannot be banned elsewhere because of First Amendment protection and the product is legally sold everywhere.

When the government adopted legislation to ban the broadcast advertising of cigarettes, this was an act of censorship that underscored in concrete terms the relationship between Congress and the broadcaster. Regardless of the issues that surrounded the passage of this legislation, the final result was censorship. The commercial broadcaster was restrained from advertising cigarettes. To do so would be to violate federal law and risk the distinct possibility of losing a means of livelihood, the license to broadcast as a business.

And this, like any and all legislation, was passed in the public interest. It is highly unlikely one would find a congressman who would admit to passing legislation that was *not* in the public interest. Therefore, this ban on advertising over the air constituted an act of censorship in the public interest.

Before continuing, it is important to remember that this was an act of censorship *by the government*. As private commercial operators, broadcasters have the right to decide what programs to air, just as publishers have the right to decide what stories to print. Such activity is an "editing" process that lies outside government jurisdiction and is *not* covered by any constitutional restriction. Of course, laws exist to protect the right of privacy—copyright—and one can sue for libel and slander, but that comes *after* the broadcast or published story.

To continue. In forbidding Congress from imposing limits on the freedom of expression, our founding fathers must have realized that in order to preserve such a freedom certain risks had to be accepted. Some citizens would inevitably take advantage of First Amendment protection. Certainly, the history of yellow journalism is a case in point. It may be suggested that this phase of journalism flourished because the public was interested in reading it, proving in one sense that this reporting was in the public interest!

This leads us to what must have been our founding fathers' perception of the First Amendment. In a representative democracy, the possible harm of damaging information was more than compensated for by the potential diversity of expression. Such diversity would contribute to the recognition of the sanctity of the individual citizen, to the discovery of truth, and to the stability of a nation founded upon the free exchange of ideas. They voted on the side of freedom of expression, unfettered by government. Perhaps they may have felt that the community and the individual should take action on a *social* rather than a political level to control undesirable expression.

Bringing up such issues as national security, the ban against yelling "fire" in a crowded theater, or any other similar concerns, where legal limits have been determined, does not invalidate the principle. There have been limited governmental and legal response to First Amendment rights in terms of national survival and causing riots, but these are individual and clearly exceptional cases, not the rule. In fact, they reinforce the validity of the First Amendment by virtue of the careful reasoning that led to those decisions. And remember, Congress has also passed the Freedom of Information Act, which to some extent draws back the cloak of government secrecy.

The point to be made is that the broadcaster as the operator of a private commercial enterprise is entitled to the same First Amendment protection as any other private enterprise. Scarcity of spectrum space (with approximately 10,000+ radio stations, 1,000+ television stations, and 7,800 cable systems with an average of about thirty channels—not to mention satellites and VCR's), can hardly be sufficient justification to go beyond technical regulation. Consider also that approximately 99 percent of U.S. homes are radio equipped, that there are an additional 137 million radio sets outside the home. Some 98 percent of U.S. homes have television with 47 percent linked to cable systems. In no other age has there ever been so much access to so many sources of information.

It is in the public interest for broadcasting, from which the public readily admits it receives the overwhelming majority of its news, to be treated differently from its First Amendment brethren in the printed media?[1] Through the years those who have opposed complete broadcast deregulation have used the theory that anyone can start a newspaper if they own a printing press, but the broadcast spectrum is limited by its scarcity. That argument simply doesn't "wash" in today's world. In mid-size communities where there are no more than one daily newspaper, as many as eight to ten radio stations and three or four television signals—and numerous cable channels—serve the population.

Those same objectors to treating the broadcaster like the printed press under the First Amendment, also raise the issue of the newspapers' Op-Ed page, a place where the citizen can speak out and voice opinions. How many letters to the editor are printed daily in newspapers across the country as opposed to those who can call in on their local radio station's talk show, or even speak with national leaders and opinion makers on such national forums as the "Larry King Show"?

Further, federal regulation of programming as it presently exists cannot be reasonably explained in the context of what the first Congress must have thought when they agreed to the First Amendment. Certainly they had to have been aware of how controversial publishing could be, but still chose to lay down the dictum that "Congress shall pass no laws."

Broadcasters as a group—and here we are describing management and ownership—are considered by and large, upper-middle-class and well educated and, as we have seen, immersed in their communities.

Over the years they have accepted their roles as public trustees even while they disputed the premise of a publicly owned spectrum.

Broadcasters are also perceived to be powerful in their influence with lawmakers. Probably nothing can be further from the truth. While perception may be considered in many cases more important than reality, here only the perception exists. Broadcasters (and this does not include their state or national associations) have been timid for the most part in lobbying their own causes or putting vast sums of money into political action committees, unlike many other professional groups.

The reason? Right or wrong, many broadcasters have seen such activity as a conflict of interest. They are so aware of their public responsibilities that it often overwhelms their own professional interests. Newspaper owners and publishers have never had that problem—witness such powerful opinion makers as the Hearsts, McCormicks, and Grahams. Many broadcasters find it difficult to divorce their news operations from their business operations in their own minds, even though the broadcast news operation exists in its own enclave, separate and independent from the rest of the station's operations. The "news room" exists as if in a hospital isolation ward, surrounded by influence on the outside by untouched by it.

If we were to imagine for a moment that Congress decided to withdraw entirely from any attempt to regulate programming, or that Supreme Court decided that the broadcaster was entirely protected by the First Amendment, what would happen? Not much. It should be apparent from the preceding articles that the public interest obligation is not an abstract principle but sound business practice for the broadcaster who must prosper in a competitive society. The marketplace, the community, professional standards, ethical considerations, social concerns all play an important role in programming standards and would predictably continue to do so.

Of course, there would be exceptions. There always have been and are now, but by far the vast majority of broadcasters continue to be guided most directly by what they must do as responsible members in their communities. And this is not an idle observation. Since broadcasting is public communication, community standards cannot be ignored without serious consequences, economic and otherwise. The broadcaster is well aware of the tension, the delicate relationship, between operating a commercially profitable business and serving the public interest.

Another area of public interest that is often overlooked is the involvement of the state and national broadcast associations in areas of public interest. This involvement can be described in many ways.

The battle against drug and alcohol abuse has been led by the state and national associations. The National Association of Broadcasters is involved in trying to foster minority ownership in broadcasting. Thirty-two state associations across the nation are involved in intern programs and scholarships, as well as broadcast seminars at colleges and universities.

Several are involved in special programs that go far beyond the public service announcement broadcast on the air. One such program can be found in Illinois where the broadcast association has developed a unique program to train air personalities as public speakers in the fight against drug abuse, alcohol, and tobacco usage. The program allows each participating station become an integral part of the anti-drug and alcohol abuse programs in their own communities and used the built-in credibility and recognition factor of their personalities to bring home these messages to diverse groups. In this particular program the association is aided by an insurance company (Country Companies Insurance, Bloomington, Illinois) and health organizations such as the American Heart Association.

Forty-three state associations sponsor awards competitions, and most include categories such as news and public affairs programs and public service announcements. Although the torch carried by these associations is not connected directly to any tower or transmitter, it is the dollars and dedication of its members that make these public interest projects work. None of these activities directly benefit individual stations as far as their public interest commitments for the record are concerned.

The articles in this book revolve around two basic themes, regardless of their content, be it a personal account, a legal treatise, or theoretical analysis. Sometimes tacitly assumed, sometimes explicitly stated, these themes form a strong undercurrent. The first is the compelling concern for freedom of expression. One perspective might openly call for greater freedom, but more often than not, the concern has been expressed by describing exemplary efforts to be creative, responsible, and responsive to community needs.

And these efforts go beyond just establishing a good performance record for license renewal time. It seems that when truly caught up in community activities, the broadcaster like any other business person realizes that an investment must be made in the welfare of the community if the station is to thrive. Public interest thus becomes the end product of sound business practice. Profit and public interest are two sides of the same coin.

The second basic theme is accountability. Broadcasting is probably the most visible commercial enterprise because it must attract attention to itself to be successful. A mistake in programming is far more likely to attract public attention than a poor tune-up job or the sale of a tight-fitting pair of shoes.

Is it not interesting that there are professional media critics for film and television, but there are no professional newspaper critics to comment on a regular basis on layout, front page content, the general quality of coverage, and other aspects? Nor are there popular critics publicly expressing their opinions about contractors, plumbers, auto mechanics, and you add the rest. If a program is unsatisfactory, one can change to another station, and if this is done by a sufficient number, the program disappears. Newspapers, however, are a much scarcer source of information without the intense competition most broadcasters face. As a result, the public has come to tolerate a wider divergence of quality without serious complaint. The point here is that accountability for the broadcasters is much more immediate and pressing.

One could apply the analogy of scales to the broadcast industry, with public interest as the structure supporting accountability on one side and profitability on the other. When the balance is achieved between accountability and profitability, the broadcaster succeeds by serving the community that, in turn, supports the station. One might ask if the community is served well enough to allow the broadcaster to thrive, why should there be additional federal intervention other than to assure a clear signal, free of interference? Could the scale of accountability and profitability be properly balanced if the FCC regulated only the technical parameters? Many broadcasters think so!

Notes

1. See the reports by the Roper Organization, Inc., including *Public Attitudes Toward Television and Other Media in a Time of Change* (New York: Television Information Office, May 1985), 16–19.

SELECTED
BIBLIOGRAPHY

Interpretations of the broadcaster's public interest obligation are prolific and diverse. This selected bibliography is designed to offer a broad spectrum of perspectives and concepts related to public interest, from economic to political, from social to legal, from programming to media ethics. Some of these works relate the issues directly to broadcasting, while others refer to the mass media in general. Sometimes the television networks become the primary focus. At other times, broadcast news is highlighted. Some books are devoted entirely to public interest issues while others address those issues as part of a broader perspective. For background purposes, some works on the history of American broadcasting have been included. It is hoped that this bibliography will be sufficiently wide-ranging to serve a variety of uses.

Abel, Elie. *What's News: The Media in American Society*. San Francisco: Institute for Contemporary Studies, 1981.

Altheid, David L. *Media Power*. Beverly Hills: Sage, 1985.

Altschull, J. Herbert. *Agents of Power: The Role of the News Media in Human Affairs*. New York: Longman, 1984.

Bagdikian, Ben H. *The Media Monopoly*. Boston: Beacon Press, 1982.

Ball-Rockeach, Sandra J. *The Great American Values Test: Influencing Behavior and Belief Through Television*. New York: Free Press, 1984.

Barcus, F. Earle. *Images of Life on Children's Television: Sex Roles, Minorities, and Families*. New York: Praeger, 1983.

Barnouw, Eric. *A Tower in Babel: A History of Broadcasting in the United States to 1933*. New York: Oxford University Press, 1966.

———. *The Golden Web: A History of Broadcasting in the United States, 1933–1953*. New York: Oxford University Press, 1968.

———. *The Image Empire: A History of Broadcasting in the United States since 1953*. New York: Oxford University Press, 1970.

————. *Tube of Plenty: The Development of American Television*. New York: Oxford University Press, 1975.

————. *The Sponsor: Notes on a Modern Potentate*. New York: Oxford University Press, 1978.

Baughman, James L. *Television's Guardians: The FCC & the Politics of Programming, 1958–1967*. Knoxville: University of Tennessee Press, 1985.

Bensman, Marvin R. *Broadcast Regulation: Selected Cases and Decisions*. Lanham, Md.: University Press of America, 1985.

Berger, Arthur A. *Television in Society*. New Brunswick, N.J.: Transaction Books, 1986.

Berry, Gordon L., and Claudia Mitchell-Kernan (eds.). *Television and the Socialization of the Minority Child*. New York: Academic Press, 1982.

Besen, S. M. *Misregulating Television: Network Dominance and the FCC*. Chicago: University of Chicago Press, 1984.

Botein, Michael, and David M. Rice (eds.). *Network Television and the Public Interest: A Preliminary Inquiry*. Lexington, Mass.: Lexington Books, 1981.

Bower, Robert T. *The Changing Television Audience in America*. New York: Columbia University Press, 1985.

Brogam, Patrick. *Spiked: The Short Life and Death of the National News Council*. New York: Twentieth Century Fund, 1985.

Carter, T. Barton, Marc Franklin, and Jay Wright. *The First Amendment and the Fourth Estate*, 3d ed. Mineolo, N.Y.: Foundation Press, 1985.

Chamberlin, Bill, and Charlene J. Brown. *The First Amendment Reconsidered: New Perspectives in the Meaning of Freedom of Speech and Press*. New York: Longman, 1982.

Charren, Peggy, and Martin W. Sandler. *Changing Channels: Living (Sensibly) with Television*. Reading, Mass.: Addison-Wesley, 1983.

Christensen, Mark, and Cameron Smith. *The Sweeps: Behind the Scenes in Network TV*. New York: Morrow, 1984.

Christians, Clifford G., Kim B. Rotzoll, and Mark Fackler. *Media Ethics: Cases and Moral Reasoning*. New York: Longman, 1983.

Conrad, Peter. *Television: The Medium and Its Manner*. Boston: Routledge and Kegan Paul, 1982.

Cross, Donna Woolfolk. *Media Speak: How Television Makes up Your Mind*. New York: Coward-McCann, 1983.

Czitrom, Daniel. *Media and the American Mind from Morse to McLuhan*. Chapel Hill: University of North Carolina Press, 1982.

Deakin, James. *Straight Stuff: The Reporters, the White House and the Truth*. New York: William Morrow, 1984.

Dennis, Everette E., and John C. Merrill. *Basic Issues in Mass Communication: A Debate*. New York: Macmillan Publishing Company, 1984.

Derthick, Martha, and Paul J. Quirk. *The Politics of Deregulation*. Washington, D.C.: Brookings Institution, 1985.

DeVol, Kenneth (ed.). *Mass Media and the Supreme Court: The Legacy of the Warren Years*. New York: Hastings House, 1982.

Diamond, Edwin, and Stephen Bates. *The Spot: The Rise of Political Advertising on Television*. Cambridge, Mass.: MIT Press, 1984.

Didsbury, Howard F., Jr. (ed.). *Communications and the Future: Prospects, Promises, and Problems*. Bethesda, Md.: World Future Society, 1982.

Dizard, Wilson P. *The Coming Information Age: An Overview of Technology, Economics, and Politics*, 2d ed. New York: Longman, 1985.

Drechsel, Robert E. *News Making in the Trial Courts*. New York: Longman, 1983.

Eastman, Susan Tyler, Sydney Head, and Lewis Klein. *Broadcast Programming: Strategies for Winning Television and Radio Audiences*, 5th ed. Belmont, Calif.: Wadsworth, 1985.

Fowles, Jib. *Television Viewers vs. Media Snobs*. New York: Stein & Day, 1982.

Fox, Stephen. *The Mirror Makers: A History of American Advertising and Its Creators*. New York: Morrow, 1984.

Friendly, Fred W. *Due to Circumstances beyond our Control*. New York: Random House, 1967.

————.*The Good Guys, the Bad Guys, and the First Amendment: Free Speech vs. Fairness in Broadcasting*. New York: Random House, 1976.

Garay, Ronald. *Congressional Television: A Legislative History*. Westport, Conn.: Greenwood Press, 1984.

Gerbner, George, and Marsha Siefert (eds.). *World Communications: A Handbook*. New York: Longman, 1984.

Gillmor, Donald M., and Jerome A. Barron. *Mass Communication Law: Cases and Comment*, 4th ed. St. Paul, Minn.: West, 1984.

Gitlin, Todd. *Inside Prime Time*. New York: Pantheon, 1983.

Glatzer, Hal. *Who Owns the Rainbow? Conserving the Radio Spectrum*. Indianapolis: Howard W. Sams, 1984.

Haigh, Robert W., George Gerbner, and Richard B. Byrne. *Communications in the Twenty-First Century*. New York: John Wiley & Sons, 1981.

Hallin, Daniel C. *The "Uncensored War:" The Media and Vietnam*. New York: Oxford University Press, 1986.

Hanhardt, John G. (ed.). *Video Culture: A Critical Investigation*. Layton, Utah: Gibbs M Smith, 1987.

Hill, George H. *Airwaves to the Soul: The Influence and Growth of Religious Broadcasting in America*. Saratoga, Calif.: R. and E. Publishers, 1983.

Himmelstein, Hal. *Television Myth and the American Mind*. New York: Praeger, 1984.

Horsfeld, Peter G. *Religious Television: The American Experience*. New York: Longman, 1984.

Hulteng, John L. *The Messenger's Motives*. Englewood Cliff, N.J.: Prentice-Hall, 1984.

————, and Roy Paul Nelson. *The Fourth Estate: An Informal Appraisal of the News and Opinion Media*, 2d ed. New York: Harper & Row, 1983.

Irwin, Manley R. *Telecommunications America: Markets without Boundaries*. Westport, Conn.: Quorum Books/Greenwood Press, 1984.

Iyegar, Shauto, and Donald R. Kinder. *News that Matters: Television & American Opinion*. Chicago: University of Chicago Press, 1987.

Jamieson, Kathleen H. *Packaging the Presidency: A History and Criticism of Presidential Campaign Advertising*. New York: Oxford University Press, 1984.

Kahn, Frank J. (ed.). *Documents of American Broadcasting*, 4th ed. Englewood Cliffs, N.J.: Prentice-Hall, 1984.

Kirkley, Donald. *Station Policy and Procedures: A Guide for Radio*. Washington, D.C.: National Association of Broadcasters, 1985.

Krasnow, Erwin G., Lawrence D. Longley, and Herbert A. Terry. *The Politics of Broadcast Regulation*, 3d ed. New York: St. Martin's Press, 1982.

Kuhn, Raymond (ed.). *The Politics of Broadcasting*. New York: St. Martin's Press, 1985.

Lang, Kurt and Gladys E. Lang (eds.). *Politics & Television Re-Viewed*. Newbury Park, Calif.: Sage, 1984.

Lesher, Stephan. *Media Unbound: The Impact of Television Journalism on the Public*. Boston: Houghton Mifflin, 1982.

Lowery, Shearon, and DeFleur, Melvin L. *Milestones in Mass Communication Research: Media Effects*, 2d ed. New York: Longman, 1988.

MacDonald, J. Fred. *Blacks and White TV: Afro-Americans in Television since 1948*. Chicago: Nelson-Hall, 1983.

———. *Television & the Red Menace: The Video Road to Vietnam*. New York: Praeger, 1985.

Madsen, Arch. *60 Minutes: The Power and Politics of America's Most Popular TV News Show*. New York: Dodd, Mead, 1984.

Marc, David. *Demographic Vistas: Television in American Culture*. Philadelphia: University of Pennsylvania Press, 1984.

Matusow, Barbara. *The Evening Stars*. New York: Ballantine Books, 1983.

Meyrowitz, Joshua. *No Sense of Place: The Impact of Electronic Media on Social Behavior*. New York: Oxford University Press, 1985.

National News Council. *In The Public Interest: A Report by the National News Council 1973–1975*. New York: The National News Council, 1975.

———. *In The Public Interest II: A Report by the National News Council, 1975–1978*. New York: The National News Council, 1979.

———. *In The Public Interest III: A Report by the National News Council, 1979–1983*. New York: The National News Council, 1984.

Newcomb, Horace (ed.). *Television: The Critical View*, 4th ed. New York: Oxford University Press, 1987.

Nimmo, Dan, and Combs, James E. *Mediated Political Realities*. New York: Longman, 1983.

———. *Nightly Horrors: Crisis Coverage in Television Network News*. Knoxville: University of Tennessee Press, 1985.

Noam, Eli M. (ed.). *Video Media Competition: Regulation, Economics, and Technology*. New York: Columbia University Press, 1985.

Parenti, Michael. *Inventing Reality: The Politics of Mass Media*. New York: St. Martin's Press, 1986.

Pell, Eve. *The Big Chill: How the Reagan Administration, Corporate American and Religious Conversations Are Subverting Free Speech and the Public Right to Know*. Boston: Beacon Press, 1984.

Pool, Ithiel de Sola. *On Free Speech in an Electronic Age: Technologies of Freedom*. Cambridge, Mass.: The Belknap Press of Harvard University Press, 1983.

Postman, Neil. *The Disappearance of Childhood*. New York: Delacorte, 1982.

Powell, Jon T. *International Broadcasting by Satellite: Issues of Regulation, Obstacles to Communication.* Westport, Conn.: Greenwood Press, 1985.

Rowan, Ford. *Broadcast Fairness: Doctrine, Practice, Prospects.* New York: Longman, 1984.

Rowland, Willard. *The Politics of TV Violence: Policy Uses of Communication Research.* Beverly Hills, Calif.: Sage, 1983.

Salvaggio, Jerry L. (ed.). *Telecommunications: Issues and Choices for Society.* New York: Longman, 1983.

Schiller, Dan. *Objectivity and the News: The Public and the Rise of Commercial Journalism.* Philadelphia: University of Pennsylvania Press, 1981.

Schubert, Glendon. *The Public Interest.* Glencoe, Ill.: The Free Press of Glencoe, 1960.

Schultze, Quentin J. *Television: Manna from Hollywood?* Grand Rapids, Mich.: Zondervan, 1987.

Schwartz, Tony. *Media: The Second God.* New York: Anchor, 1983.

Shearer, Benjamin F., and Huxford, Marilyn. *Communications and Society: A Bibliography on Communications Technologies and Their Social Impact.* Westport, Conn.: Greenwood Press, 1983.

Shudson, Michael. *Advertising, The Uneasy Persuasion: Its Dubious Impact on American Society.* New York: Basic Books, 1984.

Signorielli, Nancy. *Role Portrayal and Stereotyping on Television.* Westport, Conn.: Greenwood Press, 1985.

Smith, Leslie. *Perspectives on Radio and Television.* New York: Harper & Row, 1985.

Stevens, John D. *Shaping the First Amendment.* Beverly Hills, Calif.: Sage Publications, 1982.

Tan, Alexis S. *Mass Communication Theories and Research,* 2d ed. New York: John Wiley & Sons, 1985.

Van Der Voort, T. H. *Television Violence: A Child's View.* New York: Elsevier, 1986.

Westin, Av. *Newswatch: How TV Decides the News.* New York: Simon & Schuster, 1982.

Williams, Frederick. *The Communications Revolution,* rev. ed. New York: New American Library, 1983.

Wilson, Clint C., and Felix Gutierrez. *Minorities and Mass Media: Diversity and the End of Mass Communication.* Beverly Hills, Calif.: Sage, 1985.

Winship, Michael. *Television: A History of One of the Most Extraordinary Revolutions of All Time.* New York: Random, 1988.

INDEX